# Contents

# ST. BENEDICT
# FOR THE LAITY

Eric Dean

THE LITURGICAL PRESS
Collegeville, Minnesota 56321

Cover design by Br. Joshua Jeide, O.S.B.

The stone sculpture of St. Benedict depicted on the cover was executed by Jaume Clavell Nogueras, Barcelona, Spain; St. John's Abbey collection, Collegeville, Minnesota.

The quotations from the *Rule* in this book are from *RB 1980: The Rule of St. Benedict*, published by The Liturgical Press to celebrate the sesquimillennium of the birth of Saints Benedict and Scholastica.

Printed in the United States of America.

| | | | | | |
|---|---|---|---|---|---|
| 4 | 5 | 6 | 7 | 8 | 9 |

**Library of Congress Cataloging-in-Publication Data**

Dean, Eric, 1924–
    St. Benedict for the laity / Eric Dean.
       p.    cm.
    Includes bibliographical references.
    ISBN 0-8146-1595-3
    1. Benedict, Saint, Abbot of Monte Cassino.  Regula.  2. Christian
life—Catholic authors.  I. Title.  II. Title: Saint Benedict for
the laity.
BX3004.A2    1989b
255'.106—dc20                  89-12651
                                    CIP

A crucial turning point in . . . history occurred when men and women of good will turned aside from the task of shoring up the Roman *imperium* and ceased to identify the continuation of civility and moral community with the maintenance of that *imperium*. What they set themselves to achieve instead—often not recognizing fully what they were doing—was the construction of new forms of community within which the moral life could be sustained so that both morality and civility might survive the coming ages of barbarism and darkness. . . . [W]e ought to conclude that for some time now we too have reached that turning point. What matters at this stage is the contruction of local forms of community within which civility and the intellectual and moral life can be sustained through the new dark ages which are already upon us. And if the tradition of the virtues was able to survive the horrors of the last dark ages, we are not entirely without grounds for hope. This time however the barbarians are not waiting beyond the frontiers; they have already been governing us for quite some time. And it is our lack of consciousness of this that constitutes part of our predicament. We are waiting not for a Godot, but for another—doubtless very different—St. Benedict.

Alasdair MacIntyre
*After Virtue,* p. 263

# INTRODUCTION

Perhaps because they did not grow up near grandparents or aunts and uncles, our children had never been particularly outgoing with visitors to the house. Not that they were unfriendly. Rather, like our Cairn terrier, it was as if they wanted to make a fair judgment about persons before taking any irrevocable step toward them. I was amazed, therefore, when our youngest readily climbed up into the lap of Father Marcian, who had unexpectedly stopped by our house one Saturday morning. Even more amazing was the length of time he sat there, listening with apt attention to Father Marcian's Bible stories. Later, I noticed the same behavior toward other visiting monks.

What was it about the monks that attracted our children? Their dress both in the cloister and outside makes them look clerical if not entirely uniform. And this kind of dress would not seem to be particularly appealing to children. People tend to think that their training and lifestyle must guarantee that all monks and nuns are pretty much alike. It's the kind of thing that, based on the clothing, a child might assume. As I have come to know them, however, men and women in monastic life seem to me more diverse than any other groups of people I know. They are the last among us living in single-sex institutions, but they certainly do not have a uniform personality. Of course, my children knew nothing of these aspects of religious life. They just found Father Marcian and the other monks who came by the house very attractive.

This was doubly underlined for me at the death of Fr. Kieran Conley, one of my friends from St. Meinrad Archabbey in southern Indiana. My wife and I, not having a baby sitter available, took four-year-old Jonathan with us to St. Meinrad for the funeral. Jonathan was introduced to some monks when we arrived, and in the fashion of the young child, he volunteered that he wished his name were the same as the man whose funeral we were attending. ''Oh, you wish your name was 'Kieran?' '' someone asked. ''No, 'Conley,' '' he replied. Parents wonder about such things.

I noticed a similar phenomenon when Sr. Benedicta Ward visited our campus for a couple of weeks. She was never out and about the campus but there were several young men (all of our students are males) engaged in talking with her. What gained the students' attention was, I am sure, not the mere curiosity of a nun who teaches at Oxford, though there must have been some of that. Rather, it seemed to be the case that a person who obviously is devoting her whole life to religion constitutes something of a challenge to the assumptions with which young people have grown up in recent years. Given that young people, if they are genuinely to mature, must do quite a bit of challenging the assumptions of their elders, one could imagine the importance to them of the kind of challenge that the religious habit suggests.

One thing leading to another, I wondered whether there could be aspects of the religious life that might be available to those of us—perhaps somewhat older than undergraduates—who, for good enough reasons, are not free to go off and assume a celibate, monastic existence.

It is perhaps not so easy to visit a monastery today as it might have been in the late Middle Ages when there were many more monasteries per thousand of the population than there are today. When I talk to students about visiting a monastery, if they have any independent ideas of what to expect, I find that they imagine it to be a kind of ecclesiastical museum: a place where ancient music is to be heard and a form of life to be observed that, for all that it may have changed since the Second Vatican Council, recalls aspects of life suggestive of the Middle Ages.

In fact, there is hardly ever a day when most monasteries do not have at least a handful of visitors. But to be a visitor means that later I shall be leaving the monastery, and as I leave, I realize that there is much about the monastic life that I cannot take with me: principally the community itself, but also the schedule, the music, the location. After a number of visits, it occurred to me that I might at least read St. Benedict's *Rule for Monasteries* with some care and attention to detail.

Clearly there are many aspects of the monastic life that are not available to me, nor is the monastic life itself. The cardinal fact is that I do not have a vocation to such a life. And there is no ready way for me to take my life's work and transfer it to just any monastic community. But I found myself wondering what in St. Benedict's *Rule* might be available to secular persons living in the concluding years of the twentieth century. Though I am obviously not free to spend several hours each day following the monastic Office, are there things about the teachings and "the daily round and common task" of monastic life that might be applicable to my life?

Returning from an extended stay at Mount Saviour Monastery just outside Elmira, New York, I thought it seemed like a good idea to write down some reflections on the *Rule* in relation to my own life and concerns. A number of people, many of them in no way familiar with monasticism, read the early versions of the manuscript. Their reactions suggested I was not alone in thinking that *The Rule of St. Benedict* had things of value to say to those of us who could never actually live the monastic life.

The *Rule of St. Benedict* is one of the most important documents in the cultural history of the West. Originally written for a small Italian monastery, it immediately began to be adopted by other monastic houses. Thus it became influential throughout the Western part of the Roman Empire. In the course of the next five centuries it became, to all intents and purposes, *the* rule for monasteries in the West. In centuries before our own, men and women living under the *Rule of St. Benedict* numbered in the thousands. Although there are many fewer today than in, say, the eleventh and twelfth centuries, it is still true that hundreds of men and women of our own generation are living lives guided by the genius of this little-known Italian, St. Benedict.

Most of us educated in the twentieth century are unaware of the incredible contributions to history and culture by the heirs of St. Benedict during what have—unjustly— been called the Dark Ages and the centuries that followed. After the decline of the Roman Empire and the virtual disappearance of towns, monasteries constituted the centers of civilized living throughout Europe. Many of the little communities that grew up around monasteries became the new towns of the new European states. Perhaps most remarkable of all, the monasteries, through their copying of manuscripts, preserved a major part of what we possess of the literature of the ancient world, both Christian and pagan.

From the *Rule* itself we can infer some of the elements that made Benedictinism unique. At the time of St. Benedict, monks followed a variety of lifestyles. Some lived as hermits, some in communities. While many hermits lived sober lives, some lived in such bizarre ways that they were famous. Monastics who lived in communities did so in widely differing fashions. There do not seem to be any characteristics common to these Christian monastics except their devotion to prayer and the psalms. In particular, St. Benedict disliked those monks who perpetually drifted from house to house. Thus came the style of Benedictine monasticism: monks would live together, promised to stay together for life. Bothered by abuses that stemmed from begging for a livelihood and the luxuriousness that came from accepting gifts that made work unnecessary, St. Benedict wanted the monks who chose to be bound by his *Rule* to both pray and work. *Ora et Labora,* together with *Pax,* the classical invocation of peace, became the principal mottoes of the Benedictines.

Anyone who wishes to know more about the history of the Benedictines and of the other monastics of the West associated with the Benedictines can hardly do better than start with Dom David Knowles's often reprinted fine little book, *Christian Monasticism* (New York: McGraw-Hill, 1960). Further suggested readings are given at the end of this book.

If only because of its overwhelming significance, it could be argued that we should be familiar with the *Rule of St. Benedict.* It is, of course, a historical document, readable on its own terms. Without any particular introduction or obligation, undergraduates read it with fascination. It gives us a picture of how life was organized and what was considered important in those distant times.

The special point of this work, however, lies in my conviction that the *Rule* is still a powerful document and that it has important things to say to those of us who, because we are already committed to lives in the secular sphere, can never think of a monastic vocation. The *Rule* can speak to us of values that, even apart from the daily structures of monastic life, are relevant to our own lives in "the outside world."

Along with each heading, I suggest chapters from the *Rule* to read. It would be useful to have read through the entire *Rule* before starting to read it along with me. It does not take long to read in its entirety, especially if one does not stop to work out all the details concerning the recitation of psalms. As will become clear, this is unnecessary.

Some people have remarked that the *Rule,* for all its

genius, is a somewhat disorganized document. Others will think that some chapters could have been better located. In what follows, I begin with the topics as they occur in the *Rule* but very soon take up my own order of things. At least I end at the same place as St. Benedict.

People have been writing commentaries on the *Rule* for centuries, and I do not suppose that anything I have to say is of significant originality. The principal value of this effort will be that it encouraged some to read the *Rule* who might not otherwise have done so. As with a sermon, one hopes that one's readers or hearers will soon get back to the original text.

This is written out of the deepest affection for the monks I have been privileged to know in my thirty years of visiting monasteries. My indebtedness to them can never be adequately expressed. I shall always think first of the monks of St. Meinrad, the first abbey I ever visited and one I have been blessed to continue visiting, and then of my *fraters* of Mount Saviour Monastery, whom I can visit less often but who have taught me so much of the Christian life as it is known to St. Benedict's sons and daughters.

Some of what I write comes from my experience of living in monasteries, some from study of the writings of people who know the *Rule* and Benedictine life much more intimately than I. When I remember the source of a particular idea, I have acknowledged it, but—as with the monks themselves—my indebtedness cannot be fully acknowledged.

I owe much to my colleagues at Wabash College in Crawfordsville, Indiana. The community we are blessed to share must have been sore tested by my constant talk about monastic life. The readers of this work and I owe a debt to my Sunday school class at the Wabash Avenue Presbyterian Church, who read the first version of the manuscript. Nedra Bloom and the readers at The Liturgical Press helped make the entire work more significant and more readable.

# I

# LIFE AS SCHOOLING

## Reading from the *Rule:* Prologue, Chapter 1

Listen carefully . . . to the master's instructions, and attend to them with the ear of your heart (*RB* Prologue 1).

Do not be daunted immediately by fear and run away from the road that leads to salvation. It is bound to be narrow at the outset. But as we progress in this way of life and in faith, we shall run on the path of God's commandments, our hearts overflowing with the inexpressible delight of love (*RB* Prologue 48-49).

**W**e sometimes seek to gain a person's attention by saying firmly—rudely?—"Listen!" Rudely, because in many circumstances, the word implies a kind of superiority. Once we become aware of the way such an admonition sounds to another, we are inclined to use it less often. Only once did I snap my fingers to get the attention of our children in the hearing of my wife. But I have an uncomfortable feeling that this "Listen" is rather like snapping one's fingers to get the dog's attention. So it is strange to hear St. Benedict opening his *Rule for Monasteries* with a phrase that sounds even sharper than a mere "Listen": "Listen carefully, my son, to the master's instructions."

This opening suggests that we shall find the *Rule* going rather against our grain, as we bridle over the notion that another has authority over us. First, it is called a "rule," and we are a generation that seeks to avoid doing what we are ordered to do. Then, it starts with a call for our attention that seems more than a little brusque and seems to assert that we have a master before we are willing to acknowledge any such thing.

But as verse 2 of the Prologue suggests, St. Benedict is not claiming to be our master. Even St. Paul, as we read in verse 31, "refused to take credit for the power of his preaching." For St. Benedict, God alone is the master. His work differs in this respect from that of the "Master" whose earlier document is the source for the structure and many details of St. Benedict's *Rule*. The Master speaks forcefully in his own voice. St. Benedict speaks as a confrere of others who seek to be on their way to the heavenly city. Yet an authority rings through his words—the kind of authority our generation longs for even as it seeks to deny the domination that comes from power.

The civil rights' and women's movements in particular have made us extremely sensitive to the kinds of domination that run through our society. One does not have to sympathize with every protest to acknowledge that domination does exist. Yet we should note that much of the domination we resent in our society is associated with power rather than authority.

Clearly, we have largely lost our comprehension of the distinction, common to writers of the Middle Ages, that stands as one of the authentic achievements of the natural law tradition: the distinction between authority and power. Power is the simple exercise of force or the credible threat of force. Some suggest that a government is able to rule a nation because it has command over the military and police forces. Perhaps this is, in the end, the final vesting of the government's ability to rule. However, because of their size, police forces in most communities are quite incapable of restraining more than a small percentage of the population from violent acts. In other words, our police can keep order among us because most of us tend to be law abiding: we have respect for authority.

Perhaps the most despairing commentary on our times is that our legislators—and surely we are all associated with them in this—tend to think that more force and longer prison sentences must be the way to deal with intransigent criminals in our society. This is the appeal to power, yet we readily see that this is a failing policy. More prisons, longer and harsher sentences, only call to our attention waning respect for authority among huge segments of our population. Through the employment of increasing force to achieve social ends, we are bound to discover that force is useful only over short periods of time. With children, for example, spanking becomes no longer useful when the children are large enough that the hand of the spanker is hurt in the process. The same is true of the civil community at large. Continued use of force is the counsel of despair. A society that hopes to retain a degree of civility must depend more on authority than on power.

In certain situations, no power exists that is sufficient to gain the necessary cooperation if the individuals are unwilling. When military officers order their troops to assault an enemy position, all of whom know that it can be taken only with great loss of life, it is obvious that the officers' commands are not obeyed by reason of power or threat of force. After a court martial one might be shot for having refused to obey, but obeying will even more likely bring about one's death. Yet the orders are obeyed. Life or death situations like these make clear the difference between power and authority. Those of our citizens who have secured our freedom through their death in war are moving witnesses to what alone can maintain civil societies: respect for authority.

Of course, there are situations that suggest that power might need to be invoked to obtain compliance. But as a rough and ready proposition, it would seem that the authority persons have is inversely proportional to the amount of force they need to achieve compliance with their desires. Real authority needs no force.

It is clearly authority rather than power that lies at the heart of education. There may be some kind of learning that can be accomplished by threat of punishment. But real learning is fostered by the authority of the teacher, whose knowledge of the subject excites students and motivates them to acquire knowledge on their own behalf. It is not accidental that the qualifying degree earned by the would-be college teacher (and the only degree possessed by many of the greatest teachers in times past) is the degree of master.

One of the unfortunate manifestations of the desire for order is the focus on individuals who claim to possess a spiritual authority. One thinks of the many gurus who have established their ashrams and study centers here and there throughout the nation. Many children of the middle class have seemed to conclude that spiritual authority is found only in Eastern religious traditions. But this is not so, as the *Rule of St. Benedict* will sufficiently witness. Throughout the *Rule* itself and virtually all other monastic documents, there is clear acknowledgment that earlier monastic authorities were persons who possessed a wisdom that was readily respected, and this is no less true in our own day. One might recall the influence of Father Zossima in Dostoyevsky's *Brothers Karamazov*.

Not all persons who claim to be authoritative possess authority that Christians should acknowledge. Is their claim a desire for influence over the lives of others? A means of personal aggrandizement? Evidence of a disturbed personality? More than likely, all false claims to authority are masks for power seeking. We are reminded that we, no less than early Christians, should possess the gift of discernment. From what we read and know about St. Benedict and his work, we can conclude that nothing he says concerning authority can be construed as a desire for power.

The authority of God derives not from power but from holiness, that incredible integrity of the divine attributes that includes God's wisdom. Our own religious tradition gives recognition to an authority based upon a competence to teach and to rule that has nothing to do with power. According to the *Rule of St. Benedict,* the abbot who directs the monastery is such an authority, based on teaching and personal integrity. As we shall see, the abbot is elected by the monks, but his authority, only suggested in St. Benedict's words, "Listen carefully, my son," is founded on spiritual competence. Our ability to recognize such authority is evidence of our own developing desire for spiritual gifts.

As we begin to understand the nature of spiritual authority, we come to recognize that there are ordinary Christians among us who speak with authority, who are our teachers because of their wisdom. We have tended to think that such authority must be identified with the holding of some office. But the long experience of the Church suggests otherwise. For example, Brother Lawrence could speak of the "practice of the presence of God" while he performed only the lowliest tasks in the monastery. And the long catalog of those who were saints and martyrs is largely composed of ordinary people who possessed authority by reason of their heroic courage. Think, too, about people who, while enduring great suffering, manifest a patient acceptance of the will of God in their lives.

The psychiatrist Elisabeth Kuebler-Ross was asked by some theology students to discuss how people approach their own death. She decided instead to ask some dying patients in The University of Chicago hospitals if they would be willing to talk about their situations while the students were behind a one-way mirror. She found, to her amazement, that the patients were more than ready to do this. On the basis of this experience, she wrote an initial article, "The Dying Patient as Teacher," which later formed part of her famous book, *On Death and Dying.* Her dying patients proved to be remarkable authorities.

Who are our teachers in God? Who are the authorities, rather than the powers, in our lives?

At times of national elections, the media are full of details about the candidates' personal lives as well as their accomplishments and their liabilities. We speak of the charisma of candidates, but most of us have never realized that "charisma," the Greek word for "gift," is a word much used in New Testament discussions of the early Church. It is clear that, in elections to Church offices, the people sought to discern the gifted individuals who showed fitness for positions within the congregations and the larger community.

Realizing that "charisma" originally referred to those whom God graced with certain gifts—as opposed to those "graced" with a striking TV personality—we might take seriously the proposition that the truly charismatic among us rather than the ambitious are fitted to bear authority.

It would be difficult otherwise to understand how early bishops—or abbots—were elected.

In the school for the Lord's service that God has provided for those of us who do not live in the monastery, there are authorities equipped to speak to us of what we desire to know. Some of them, as we have said, are quite the most surprising: humble folk doing necessary tasks, people subjected to appalling suffering who have retained the grace of Christian witness. But there are also people of great social importance who accept their successes in life as a call to stewardship.

It may even be that there are gifts which are expressed other than in terms of piety or social idealism. In the Old Testament, for example, we read of "my shepherd Cyrus," an alien ruler through whom the Jews were able to return to Jerusalem and rebuild the Temple (see Isa 44:28). And so, we are called to pray for all those in authority.

It would be well if we could evaluate our own leaders in terms that make Christian sense, whether or not those individuals identify themselves in terms of ordinary pieties.

We should seek to be discerning electors, to discover among the candidates for office those gifted to speak clearly to an increasingly democratic and pluralistic society about the kinds of concerns that might bind the nation more firmly together.

Throughout our lives as Christians, what speaks to us in many lives is the kind of authority St. Benedict cites, an authority that calls us ''daily to translate into action . . . [the Lord's] holy teachings'' (*RB* Prologue 35).

''Never swerving from [the master's] instructions, then, but faithfully observing his teaching in the monastery until death, we shall through patience share in the sufferings of Christ that we may deserve also to share in his kingdom'' (*RB* Prologue 50).

# II

## ABBOT AND FATHER

**Reading from the** *Rule:* **chapters 2, 3, 21, 31, 56, 64–66**

> Everything he teaches and commands should, like the
> leaven of divine justice, permeate the minds of his disciples
> (*RB* 2:5).

For many of us, "pope" is simply the title referring to a
particularly important person, the principal bishop of the
Roman Catholic Church. We may, therefore, be surprised
to realize—perhaps as we listen to an Italian crowd acclaim-
ing a newly elected pope—that the word means simply
"papa," even "daddy." When Jesus prays to his Father in
the Garden of Gethsemane, his "abba" is this same familiar name for father.

It is hard for most of us to think that God might ever
be addressed with such a childlike word. We need to realize that "abbot," too, has this connotation. As the name
for an authoritative person, it is unfamiliar to us in its
familiarity, as are "abba" and "father."

For anyone who knows even the least amount of monastic history, the abbot, the head of the monastery, has a role
that suggests a magisterial importance. In times past, the
abbots of many of the larger and more famous monasteries
had their own houses. Sometimes the abbot was forced
upon the community, an important person in court who

held the office but who rarely appeared and was probably not even familiar with the area. At the very least, he had his own table in the refectory and invited guests to eat there with him. Abbot, we think, and we call to mind a very important person whose presence requires deference.

We might as well acknowledge that the abbacy is an authoritative role in the monastic community. St. Benedict refers to this authority repeatedly. But the authority of the abbot is always exercised for the benefit of the community. At no point does the *Rule of St. Benedict* suggest what we assume was the norm throughout the medieval period: an abbot who has to be obeyed because he is an authority in his own right. In the later period, it was common to speak of divine right, a doctrine that holds the king's authority to be his own personal inherited possession. But the rights of abbots cannot be thought of in such terms, and although some abbots and abbesses were treated as equals by powerful secular rulers (they even commanded armies), there is nothing in the *Rule* that justifies such activities.

Likewise, the attitude that we might describe as "authoritarian" has no place in the recommendations of the *Rule*. The abbot should think only of his responsibility before God for the well-being of the community under his care.

No one reading the *Rule* is likely to aspire to become the abbot of a monastery. St. Benedict's comments concerning the abbot's responsibilities are fairly awe inspiring, with no suggestion that it is an office to be assumed lightly. In any event, the abbot is only the surrogate head of the monastery; Christ is its proper head. "The abbot must, therefore, be aware that the shepherd will bear the blame wherever the father of the household finds that the sheep have yielded no profit" (*RB* 2.7). It is clear that while the abbot is answerable to no one within the monastery, he will have to answer to a righteous judge.

The magisterial abbot has largely disappeared, and recent years have seen a rediscovery of the essence of the *Rule*.

The abbot is the local father, a shepherd whose discipline is exercised for the benefit of the members of the household. His rule in the monastery stems largely from the members of the community giving him deference as holder of the office, not from the assertion of personal rights and privileges. In a large monastery, of course, the abbot has a huge variety of responsibilities, and his days are filled with correspondence and meetings. But whether the monastery is large or small, the contemporary understanding of the *Rule* casts the abbot in a role much more like that of a college dean than a corporation president. He is a monk whose responsibilities set him aside for a life of service.

In smaller monasteries where household chores can never be forgotten, it is entirely likely that the abbot will be found working alongside other members of the community, even doing work others might avoid, perhaps in the bakery or the laundry. The abbot's willingness to work suggests that we, also, ought to work willingly. I am reminded of the one-time military notion that no man should be ordered to do what the officer would be unwilling to do. This was, of course, the measure of acceptable risk. It did not imply doing the chores in the kitchen, as is the case in monasteries.

To be sure, our expectations in such matters must be reasonable. My closest observation of monastic life has been in small houses in which the abbot participates in the chores. In larger monasteries, the abbot's larger responsibilities may preclude his labor alongside his monks. In an early monastery with more than a hundred monks—of which there once were many and which are typical of most of the monasteries known to us—the overall management of monastery affairs must have demanded much of the abbot's time. Today, however, even in fairly large monasteries, the abbot will often try to do a certain amount of physical labor.

How would it be if I were to think of my role as the father of a family by analogy to the abbot's role?

We are rethinking our ideas about what constitutes true

authority as we become increasingly aware that not all families are headed by men. But much of the criticism of the so-called male-dominated family is a protest against the privilege that seems implicit: the "right" of a person to order things to his own liking. This is the kind of privilege St. Benedict's abbot might have possessed had he chosen to exercise it. Who would protest, however, if it were clear that the "right" of ordering the community stemmed not from privilege but from the assumption of responsibility, a responsibility that the rest of the community honored? Clearly, it would be a misunderstanding of the abbot's role to think that he runs the monastery to suit himself. Any objection to the manner in which an abbot runs a particular monastery would be an objection to that abbot rather than to the office as envisaged by the *Rule*. One wonders whether the same is not true of other roles seen as dominant, particularly that of husband: the objection is not to the essence of the role but the manner in which it is exercised.

The rediscovery of the role of abbot suggests that the role of head of household might also be reclaimed. It is not that the office needs to be done away with. It only needs to be better understood and exemplified.

Pope John XXIII once invited some Protestant Christians who were troubled by the office and title of "pope" to think of him in terms of the title "Servant of the Servants of God." This is reminiscent of Christ's saying that he came to minister, not to be ministered unto. How beneficial it would be if we could see that the legitimacy of true authority in human affairs stems from the willingness to be responsible for others, to serve them, even to call them to account when their own well-being is at stake. We must acknowledge that it is the exercise of responsibility on our behalf that accords others a degree of rule in our lives. As *RB* 63.13 makes clear, although the abbot is to be called "lord," this is not because he claims that title for himself. Service is not a justification for claiming to be treated with special respect.

One of the most interesting sections of the *Rule* speaks of the abbot's taking counsel from members of the community. All are to be listened to, remarkably beginning with the most junior member of the community. As we shall see, this is quite contrary to what one might expect given that members of the community are ranked by their date of profession. There may be good reason for this exception. It is difficult to imagine that the younger members would feel free to express themselves, particularly if their ideas are somewhat innovative, should their seniors already have given opinions that differ. So we should tend to say that we should not benefit from the advice of the young unless they are given first crack at speaking. Most significant, however, is the concern for the young as persons that this directive reveals. We become aware that, throughout the *Rule*, St. Benedict's ideas are marked by a particular sensitivity to personal feelings.

When consulted in this way, all should feel free to offer their views. Yet as the fine, modern Rule of Taizé and St. Benedict's *Rule* both clearly say, when the abbot has taken counsel with the brothers, he himself must decide what is right. Both rules reflect the idea, acknowledged from time to time in Western history, that democracy is not necessarily the ideal way of making decisions (although, as Churchill suggested, it may be, for nations, the least-bad way). St. Benedict realizes that we all tend to want our own say. Yet it is better that a community not be in constant turmoil because of its members soliciting one another's agreement on matters of passing importance. This manner of deciding issues leads to the development of factions. Preferable is what the *Rule* proposes: All will have their say before the community, then the abbot will make the decision. This obviously calls for respect for both the office and the responsibility entrusted to its holder.

It is noteworthy that the subordinate offices of the monastery are endorsed by St. Benedict in terms of the pastoral aspect of the abbot's role. Deans, cellarer, porter: All are to be persons, as he says specifically of the deans, "with whom the abbot can confidently share the burdens of his office. They are to be chosen for virtuous living and wise teaching, not for their rank" (*RB* 21.3-4). For the role of prior, whose office is particularly prone to temptation, St. Benedict shows special concern. Some monasteries of his time, in which both abbot and prior had been appointed by the same person from outside, apparently saw a struggle for power between abbot and prior. For this reason, St. Benedict is reluctant to endorse the office of prior without sounding many alarms. It is moving that he recognizes that the existence of the prior's office within the monastery also presents a source of temptation for the abbot: "Yet the abbot should reflect that he must give God an account of all his judgments, lest the flames of jealousy or rivalry sear his soul" (*RB* 65.22).

We have been so thoroughly imbued with arguments for democracy that we are inclined to forget its abuses. No doubt the abuses of other forms of government are worse, but the abuses of democracy can lead to an aimlessness that has little to recommend it. It is possible to spend time debating matters that are of no practical consequence but that assume such increasing symbolic significance that, at last, the community is embroiled with factions struggling for the upper hand. Clearly, factions cannot be permitted in a monastery. It would be well for us if, at large, we could acknowledge the beneficence of a wise leadership, insist upon it, perhaps—and so free ourselves to be about our essential human work.

As citizens of the United States, we would do well to recall the profound discussions conducted among the Founders concerning the form of government that should obtain in the new nation. Readers of the Federalist Papers must incline to the notion that St. Benedict would have been sympathetic with those who preferred a representative form of government over those who wished all matters to be constantly before the entire population. Few classical discussions concerning political philosophy have ever quoted St. Benedict. Clearly, as one who laid down principles for a form of community living that has proved valid through the longevity of its existence, he merits respectful attention in this regard.

Actually, of course, the single moment in the monastery that appears to be fully democratic occurs when an abbot is being elected. But even here the voting is limited to those under solemn vows, and the new abbot would ordinarily come from their number. It is a difficult issue in our political life today, but St. Benedict would seem to be of the opinion that a certain degree of experience is required in order to be a wise elector.

Acceptance of the *Rule's* principle of headship calls for us to achieve a certain spiritual maturity, whether we are called to acknowledge the headship of another or to accept the responsibilities of headship ourselves. Generally we have been led to think that a universal democratic equality is best. But to those who have experienced monastic communities, the *Rule's* requirement seems laudable: Let all have their say, then let the abbot decide. Those who bear such responsibility, however, must always recall that God is the righteous judge of their stewardship. Also, such a person, whether abbot or president or some other officer, deserves the support of our prayers.

# III

## THE TOOLS OF THE COMMUNITY

**Reading from the *Rule:*** chapters 4, 32

These, then, are the tools of the spiritual craft. When we have used them without ceasing day and night and have returned them on judgment day, our wages will be the reward the Lord has promised: *What the eye has not seen nor the ear heard, God has prepared for those who love him* (1 Cor 2:9) (*RB* 4.75–77).

The *Rule's* first mention of tools is in chapter 4, which is entitled "The Tools for Good Works" and deals with behavior that helps build up the monastery. But the reference to the return of the tools (*RB* 4.76) anticipates chapter 32 in which there is talk of the care and storing of the workmen's tools of the monastery. It can hardly be accidental that St. Benedict uses the same term to refer both to proper behavior and to the instruments for the physical work of the monastery. So there are two kinds of tools for which we ought to be concerned.

The principal kind of tools are those of chapter 4: the attitudes toward one another that build up the community, an apt concern for one's own character, and the concern for one another "in the workshop where we are to toil faithfully'' (*RB* 4.78). One of the unfortunate developments of our time is that these attitudes have come to be regarded as techniques for handling other people. Perhaps St. Benedict's use of the term ''tool'' might seem, to some, consistent with such an idea. But the attitudes that he calls ''tools'' cannot in any sense be regarded as ''techniques.'' They are, rather, the attitudes that human beings must bear toward one another.

The distinction between what are properly called ''techniques'' and the attitudes St. Benedict calls ''tools'' is worth clarifying. We have been inundated in recent years with books having in their titles the words ''how to.'' All of them are designed to enable us to better handle our lives or the people in our lives. But unlike the *Rule*, virtually every one of the ''how to'' books talks about kinds of manipulation. Some are relatively explicit. What should you say to persons to make them think that you are thoughtful, kind, and concerned for their welfare? What should you say about the awful outfit—of which its owner is obviously so proud—that will leave the owner grateful to you?

Anyone who has talked with a telephone bond-salesman may have been surprised at the ready way in which, after one has said something like, ''Well, I should certainly want to talk with my wife before making a decision,'' the person on the line has responded, ''You don't mean that your wife knows more about these things than you do?''

Although in my case the answer is sensibly yes, the form of the question was so bullying that I found myself hesitating. Thus, I was not surprised to discover that the people who work these unscrupulous telephone operations are instructed in how to stampede the man to whom they might be talking by referring to his wife in this insulting fashion. Presumably there are alternate forms when they are speaking to a married woman.

Questions asked in this fashion are devices designed to manipulate other human beings.

These questions are, I think, qualitatively different from

those which look at how to answer honestly yet avoid hurting people's feelings when they ask your opinion about aspects of themselves or their garb which perhaps to you seem inappropriate or undesirable. For the most part, we say something noncommital which avoids answering: "I'm a fine person to ask; I wear flowered ties with striped shirts."

But we all know situations in which it seems necessary to run the risk of offending. Students may prefer to have a teacher say their writing is fine, but it is neither honest nor helpful for teachers to ignore what students should learn to improve. What must be remembered is that situations like this are open to the possibility of cruelty. Frustrated over some purely personal matter, we sometimes make our suggestions more cutting than need be, even though we know well enough that "speaking the truth in love" must be carefully distinguished from willful cruelty. To be willfully cruel is to use the other person's pain to satisfy our own need. "Speaking the truth in love" can never be described in this way.

If the matter seems confused, we might remember Martin Buber's comment in his remarkable *I and Thou* that hatred is like love in that it is an attitude toward the real person. Hatred is more like love than is mere cruelty. Hatred is thus rather selective, while I might be cruel on a wide scale. It seems, incidentally, that anyone who imagines hating everyone is actually manifesting self-hatred.

Once, somewhat depressed over the poor grades that were on the tests I was returning to a class, it occurred to me to say what is undoubtedly true: "I don't have to worry about what I will say to the students who get good grades. They won't bother to come and see me. It's the students who get Ds and Fs whom I must be prepared to meet as persons who have been hurt by my estimate of their work. I had just never realized it before, but it was so obviously true and our whole relationship was changed (and incidentally, the students' work improved too).

Techniques, on the other hand, are designed to advance the interests of one person at the expense of others who are not really taken seriously as persons. The books about techniques may be successful in the market, but nothing can be said in favor of manipulating human beings. Some of us need to be guarded in our personal relationships because we are naturally rather good at it; most of us could doubtless learn to be better at it if we wanted that. In any event, the attempt to manipulate others should be distinguished from dealing with others honestly, firmly, and with their good in mind.

We must take care to assert that it is simply not true that the only way human beings ever deal with other human beings is by manipulating them. The psychology that holds this view is impoverished in every possible fashion. To be concerned for the effect of my behavior upon other people is one thing. To try to affect their behavior without their being aware of what I am doing is entirely different. The tools of the monastery must be actions concerned for the good of others: nowhere in the *Rule* is there any justification for self-satisfying actions. St. Benedict's tools are the personalized means of building up relations—as all tools become personalized through continual use.

Clearly it is important that we not carry grudges against one another, that we be truthful to one another, that we give credit to one another. All of these are the behavioral tools of which St. Benedict speaks. But they are, if one might make the distinction, hand tools rather than machines. The matter of not bearing grudges is a good case in point. There are certain kinds of personal behavior that can, so to speak, be mechanized. One thinks of the mechanical—or even intentionally cruel—exercise of "truthtelling" as it is practiced in some quarters. "Letting it all hang out," as it used to be called.

Although spreading hurtful but genuine information about another human being will not get us into court for libel or slander, a genuine concern for truth requires a concern for persons. Bonhoeffer reminds us that, except within intimate relationships (and perhaps not even then, for even within marriage there are appropriate elements of privacy), "telling the truth is not saying all you know."

But the ordinary work within intimate human communities that requires actual tools is no less vital. St. Benedict puts prayer and work side by side. We have, in our day, a tendency to place greater emphasis on some kinds of work than on others. We tend to denigrate work done around the house, as if that work did not help the family. Work done outside the home, wherever it is carried out, might also be misunderstood. Clearly, we should enhance our capacity to be marriage partners if we could acknowledge that many kinds of work are crucial to the marriage in its full complexity.

It is now considered foolish and somehow undesirable for a person to be what was once called "house-proud." God knows that there have been, perhaps still are, people who are nothing short of idolatrous toward their automobiles, their gardens, their kitchen floors or what-have-you. But idolatry apart, our relationships with one another could be significantly improved if we could recognize the whole range of tools that are used in the complete family.

It may well be the case that women who have regarded themselves comfortably as housewives were clearer on this point than were most husbands. The kind of devotion with which homes and families have traditionally been tended must often have been a tacit but loving affirmation of the relationship which was served through all of that work. And there must have been some husbands who went off to their jobs with similar thoughts about their own work. Unfortunately, it became accepted that these were two kinds of work, one drudgery and the other prestigious and unrelated to common purpose. Neither the work around the house nor the work of the workplace was seen as nurturing the marriage; for many, marriage itself has been understood as living together for no more than convenience.

There is a sounder understanding of work and marriage. The *Rule* would suggest that families and other kinds of intimate communities (even quite large communities if we have sufficient imagination and the fortitude to carry the thought through)—together with all of the kinds of work they entail—are more like organisms than they are like collections of disconnected individuals associated merely for convenience.

We are tempted to think that tools are only instruments, not the essence of our lives. It is instructive that St. Benedict says that carelessness with the tools of the monastery is to be reproved and habitual carelessness disciplined. Even things humble in appearance are symbols of the community that requires their use.

Reflection on this aspect of the *Rule* implies that we should pray for and hold in particular esteem public figures who have the integrity and personal courage to carry these values into the larger communities of life: city, state, nation, community of nations.

Through an understanding of tools, we come to understand the common purposes that are established in communities of secular life as well as in the monastic communities. Chapters 4 and 32 carry a common theme which is combined in the concluding words of chapter 4:

> These, then, are the tools of the spiritual craft. When we have used them without ceasing day and night and have returned them on judgment day, our wages will be the reward the Lord has promised: *What the eye has not seen nor the ear heard, God has prepared for those who love him* (1 Cor 2:9).
>
> The workshop where we are to toil faithfully at all these tasks is the enclosure of the monastery and stability in the community (*RB* 4.75–78).

Perhaps we should add for ourselves, "The workshop . . . is the home."

# IV

## HUMILITY

### Reading from the *Rule:* Chapters 5–7, 69–72

Through this love, all that he once performed with dread, he will now begin to observe without effort, as though naturally, from habit, no longer out of fear of hell, but out of love for Christ, good habit and delight in virtue. All this the Lord will by the Holy Spirit graciously manifest in his workman now cleansed of vices and sins (*RB* 7:68–70).

No single word is more likely to rankle us than "obedience." To readers of modern psychology textbooks, it seems a thoroughly unlikable word for a thoroughly undesirable state of mind. I don't mind thinking about an obedient dog. I may criticize a neighbor whose dog is disobedient or ill-trained. But it seems odd these days to praise children by calling them obedient; saying that an adult is obedient suggests a lack of maturity.

And if there were a word more likely to bother us than "obedience," it could well be "humility."

So we become uncomfortable as we note that while the title of chapter 5 is "Obedience," St. Benedict seems to be a bit distracted and obedience turns out to be but the first step of twelve toward the perfecting of humility.

One can imagine being obedient by reason of pressure from outside. Dogs are not long obedient unless their trainers maintain consistent pressure upon them. In other words, I might be obedient without necessarily wanting to be obedient. Obedience may, to be sure, be an attitude: I may desire to be obedient. But obedience is defined by behavior, and one could be judged obedient without ever desiring to be obedient. Humility is different. I might somehow be forced to behave as if I were humble, but the person doing the forcing would know I was not genuinely humble. Like Charles Dickens's Uriah Heep, without being truly humble, I might use an apparent humility as a means of manipulating other people.

Notice the difference: false humility like Uriah Heep's is a studied deception, but unwilling obedience is still obedience.

A soldier is not less obedient to the officer if, saying nothing, in every moment he is presenting arms or advancing on the enemy he wishes he might be doing otherwise. Obedience is defined by behavior. I can't ever be entirely sure that the person I think of as humble *is* humble, but he commits a substantial deception if he is not what he seems. In ordinary human contexts, obedience is defined by the act, humility by the attitude.

It is appropriate to acknowledge that in the context of St. Benedict's monastery, obedience has a somewhat different character. Since the monastic has a duty to make his or her thought known to the abbot, there could be no private reservations concerning one's obedience. Here obedience is required as both attitude and act. While recognizing the propriety of the monastic's being open to the abbot, it is appropriate to acknowledge that a civil society would hardly be possible if we were required to make known to the authorities the attitudes behind our public behavior. This distinction is important to understanding the nature of St. Benedict's community.

It is surely the case that any discussion of virtues in our

culture today would mention courage and honesty, almost certainly sensitivity, but just as certainly *not* obedience and humility. These are attitudes that many would characterize as servile. At their mention, many tend to say ugh and seek to change the subject.

It is at the very least sobering that St. Benedict gives us three chapters devoted to topics that grate on modern sensibilities. Obedience, which comes first, seems to be the initial step toward humility, but the other steps are somehow forgotten in chapter 5. Obedience is reaffirmed, of course, in chapter 7 and appears there as the third step toward complete humility. And this angular virtue is complemented by restraint of speech and humility, developed in twelve steps. St. Benedict here seems to be wholly guided by the Rule of the Master mentioned earlier—even to following the Master's seeming forgetfulness in chapter 5.

As with other writers of monastic rules, both St. Benedict and the Master recognize that they are following the wisdom of earlier teachers on religious life, such as the noted Cassian. And St. Benedict, like his predecessors, is not disposed to be the comfortable religious teacher who merely confirms us in all our favorite attitudes of mind.

Yet if obedience, restraint of speech, and humility are an unattractive trio by contemporary standards, they may well be the key to that quiet air of self-possession that characterizes experienced monastics. Such monastics seem open and unthreatened by anyone they meet, principally, I believe, because they have been schooled not to test their worth in some kind of psychological combat. With our contemporaries, we tend to regard humility as a kind of weakness. But true humility, in practice, turns out to be the opposite: it is strength of character. St. Benedict calls these humble monastics who live in communities "the strong kind" (*RB* 1.13). For St. Augustine, to be humble is to be able to say, "I do not fear anything," and this compares with St. Benedict's reference to 1 John 4:18 "The monk will quickly arrive at that *perfect love* of God which *casts out fear*"

(*RB* 7.67). Humility is a characteristic worth thinking about.

Because of the humility that marks the community, the visitor is accepted without any kind of extended social introduction. It would seem inappropriate for the monastic to speak of self, as if to say, for example, ''I am the monk who is to be distinguished from my brothers by my particular interest in reading the Patristics.'' In much the same way, the visitor is accepted after giving no more than his name. The typical monastic greeting is ''You're Eric? I'm Brother Gregory.''

Surely the difference between such a sparse greeting and the fulsome exchanges one hears at cocktail parties is significant. Occasionally, of course, it is no more than polite to identify oneself and mention one's position or interests, but often these facts are cited as an example of what Stephen Potter used to write about voluminously: one-upmanship. A cruel example of a ploy such as is used in one-upmanship is Winston Churchill's comment about Clement Attlee: ''He is a modest man and he has much to be modest about.'' Churchill, of course, must be making a personal reference intended to be flattering to himself. One's ploys are self-references put forward to establish one's worth, to show that one is an interesting social partner—at least for the time of the party.

The humility cultivated by those living under the *Rule of St. Benedict* permits them to accept visitors as the *Rule* proposes—as if each visitor were Christ. Each person is to be valued as the unique person he or she is.

At first a visitor finds this disconcerting. We are so used to being treated in accordance with some kind of social standing, usually by reference to title or office or wealth.

Giving up these ordinary social recognition signals seems depersonalizing—almost like deprivation. This is understandable because we learn to think of ourselves in terms of our roles in society. Then we discover that being treated as oneself without reference to one's work or social position offers an opportunity for a new kind of freedom. And this freedom is one of the significant benefits we derive from visiting monasteries. We begin to grasp the nature of humility.

This clearer concept of the consequences of humility eliminates a common misunderstanding of monastic personality. For those who know litttle about monastics, it is not surprising if, upon reading St. Benedict's discusson of humility, they imagine monks to be deprived of individuality with personalities as uniform—and uninteresting?— as their uniform monastic garb might suggest. This was the reaction of one of my undergraduate students when reading the *Rule* recently. To meet just a couple of monastics is to find the contrary to be the case. My students were amazed at the way in which the monk who talked with them about the *Rule* anticipated their questions and seemed to be rather whimsically familiar with the nature of undergraduate concerns.

My St. Meinrad friend must have smiled a little when he said (in the day in which the word was current), ''I don't think people realize that monasteries are the last refuge of the *real* kooks.'' Kooks, perhaps, as defined by their love of God.

Those of us who have social titles and public roles must, on reflection, realize that much of our lives is consumed by ''acting appropriately.'' How, then, might it be to have one's character formed by an ideal that leaves one free to meet people unconstrained by such conventions? It would be the kind of freedom that is gained from being on vacation where one is unknown, the kind of freedom that would, at least momentarily, come from moving to a new job in a town where one had never lived before.

Genuine humility, however, would be a new kind of freedom: perhaps the freedom of the Christian person of whom we read in Scripture. Only by daring to desire such a virtue might we discover it. But, we find ourselves saying, what about this business of obedience?

Of course there can be problems in a monastery, just as

in any community made up of fallible human beings. Chapter 68 quite explicitly acknowledges this. No doubt there have been, and may still be, abbots who are imperious and demanding. It is important to note, however, that the obedience owed the abbot is the obedience we owe Christ: ''He is believed to hold the place of Christ in the monastery'' (RB 2.2). Recognizing that Christ is our model of humility and that obedience is owed to him and to those who represent him among us, we see that a different attitude is needed. For the monastic, obedience and humility are both external and internal acts.

Our contemporary tendency is to challenge authority. A fairly typical response to any command is, ''Who's he to tell me to do that?'' but the obedience we owe to Christ is not the grudging obedience that tends to question authority. Since he is among us in all humility, our obedience to Christ is a symbol of the deference we owe to all of our brothers and sisters.

Early Christians (see Rom 13 and Rev 13) needed to think quite hard about the nature of the claims upon them from various authorities, especially the Roman emperor. It is instructive to see that, like the Puritans in England long after them, they attempted—so far as it was possible—to behave respectfully even toward an authority that was unfriendly to them. Such a ''civil'' attitude—perhaps as it led on into ''civil disobedience'' when simple obedience was no longer possible—seems to have been a more effective way to deal with problems than outright denial of authority. The writings of spiritual teachers in the Church are full of arguments that an authority which is tending to go wrong is more likely to be reclaimed if treated with respect than if it is defied.

So with an abbot who has become arbitrary, so with a boss, a husband, a wife. . . . Is it possible that what St. Benedict is recommending is more difficult, the more intimate the relationship?

One of the strange insights afforded by the Rule comes from the reference to rank in the monastery. It seems quite arbitrary. Like the birth order of children of a natural family, a monk is ranked according to the date that he made his vows in the community. St. Benedict says that even priests who enter the monastery must be content to be ranked this way. The abbot may give a person a different rank, though it is not at all clear what this signifies. It may simply mean that the abbot may choose to give a relative newcomer some office in the community. But, in any event, all should be satisfied to be ranked according to the date of their profession and accept the fact that those who entered the community earlier are one's seniors.

The *Rule* explicitly requires a monk to address all his seniors in the monastery as "father," and this is still the practice in some monasteries. Monks have told me that this is a significant lesson, hard to learn. Imagine an educated man who enters the monastery after an unlearned man much his junior by age. To accept one's rank, reasonably defined in this way, is itself a major lesson in humility.

Abelard, who was one of the most brilliant and world-famous scholars of the twelfth century and whose works still are studied with care, ended his days in the monastery of Cluny. After his death, Peter the Venerable, abbot of Cluny, writing to Abelard's brilliant and remarkable wife Heloise about Abelard's last days, says of him:

> The nature and extent of the saintliness, humility and devotion of his life among us, to which Cluny can bear witness, cannot briefly be told. I do not remember seeing anyone, I think, who was his equal in conduct and manner: St. Germain could not have appeared more lowly nor St. Martin himself so poor. And although at my insistence he held superior rank in our large community of brothers, the shabbiness of his attire made him look the humblest of them all. I often marvelled, and when he walked in front of me with the others in the usual processional order, I almost stood still in astonishment that a man who bore so great and distinguished a name could thus humble and abase himself. And because some who profess the religious

life want unnecessary extravagance even in the habits they wear, he was completely frugal in such matters, content with a simple garment of each sort, seeking nothing more.

Thus did Master Peter end his days. He who was known nearly all over the world for his unique mastery of knowledge and who won fame everywhere as a disciple of one who said, ''Learn from me, for I am gentle and humble-hearted,'' steadfast in his own gentleness and humility, thus passed over to him.

We can only be moved as we read of Abelard, and we can try in forms appropriate to our own situation in life to exemplify what St. Benedict teaches in his *Rule* about restraint, about humility, about obedience.

# V

## SINGING THE PSALMS

### Reading from the *Rule* chapters 8–19

Let us consider, then, how we ought to behave in the presence of God and his angels, and let us stand to sing the psalms in such a way that our minds are in harmony with our voices (*RB* 19:6–7).

Understandably, laypeople are likely to find these sections of the *Rule* (chs. 8–19) of somewhat less than immediate interest. Only those who love to solve puzzles would have a particular desire to meet the challenge of the text and to work out the complex cycle of psalms St. Benedict proposes for use at the different times of the day.

When I started to visit Benedictine monasteries, I had it in mind to do a study of the Office. Although significant changes had been brought about in religious communities, it seemed to me that the Fathers of the Second Vatican Council had gone to particular pains to permit wide changes in this section of the *Rule*. Consequently, most monasteries have significantly changed the manner in which they carry out the Daily Office—their cycle of community prayer. For a variety of reasons, monasteries had found it increasingly difficult to follow the *Rule* in a literal fashion. Thus, there was considerable experimentation. The venerable melisma of Gregorian chant did not go particularly well with the now-permitted common-language text of the psalms— mostly English in the United States, French in Quebec— and there was a good bit of trying out how to arrange the sequence in which the psalms would be used. New kinds of musical settings are now common, but there are still a few monastic houses that stick closely to the hours and psalm cycles given in the *Rule*. The majority have adopted a simplified order.

Perhaps it would be useful to give a rough approxima- tion of the way in which a fairly typical monastery once would have organized its daily schedule, or *horarium*, to meet the requirements of the *Rule*. The Night Office was said in the middle of the night or perhaps quite early in the morning; the Office of Lauds was meant to be at about sun- rise and Vespers at sunset. Thus, since there were four other "hours" to be fitted between Lauds and Vespers, the time between the various "hours" varied considerably in lati- tudes with a marked difference in the length of day between summer and winter. One wonders whether St. Benedict realized that in the north of Scotland, in summer it was just getting dark at ten in the evening, yet in winter it was dark by four. In Italy the difference between summer and win- ter would not have been quite so marked.

Without taking all of these complications into account, a monastic day would have been something like the fol- lowing:

| | |
|---|---|
| Night Office Vigils | 4:00 a.m. |
| Lauds | 5:30 |
| Prime | 6:30 |
| Terce | 10:00 |
| Sext | 12:00 p.m. |
| None | 3:00 |
| Vespers | 5:30 |
| Compline | 7:00 |

To this schedule, depending on local custom, would have been added work, study, a meal or meals, and the daily celebration of Mass. Whatever else might be said about the *horarium*, the practice of rising in the "middle of the night" (at four o'clock or even at midnight) is not an incredible hardship if one has been sleeping since sundown, especially in winter in the northern latitudes. And in houses where monastics worked or studied between an early Night Office and Lauds, it would have been the practice to take a midday siesta during the very long days of summer.

It is obvious that such a schedule is a constant interruption of the other activities that need to be carried out in the monastery. If the apostolic work of the monastery is the operation of a preparational school, for example, it would be necessary to excuse numbers of monastics from several of the hours so that students might be properly supervised. Since this leaves the recitation of the Office to monastics not so engaged, the Office is no longer an action of the whole community in practice, though it remains so by intention.

Given such pressures on the day, it became increasingly common to combine hours, until now, with permission of the Fathers of the Second Vatican Council. Most larger houses, where the work of monastics may be of a number of different kinds, have reordered the Office to three times a day. Typically, there is a significant Morning Office (usually around six), a short Office at noon, and an Evening Office that combines the features of Vespers and Compline. The daily celebration of Mass is sometimes combined with one of these. Given this modification, it has become necessary to move to a two- or three-week cycle of psalms rather than the one-week cycle. This may seem like a relaxation of discipline, but St. Benedict points out that the strictest monks of his time were reciting all one hundred and fifty psalms each day, so that even his weekly cycle would have seemed like an incredible relaxation of earlier practice.

The later monks of Cluny, wanting a stricter observance

of the *Rule*, returned to the daily cycle of psalms; as a result, they were no longer able to work to the degree St. Benedict had desired for his monks. The natural consequence was that there needed to be some members of the community, called *conversi*, who were more nearly servants than monks. Their devotion to the community was, perhaps, the more admirable for the simplicity of their service.

When we propose to visit a monastery, we tend to anticipate that the Office will be burdensome. In fact, however, most people discover that it is not a burden. Accepting the discipline of getting up in the morning makes it natural to go to bed earlier; thus the day is simply reoriented. Beyond this, the routine of the Daily Office comes to be an appropriate punctuation of the day, no more irritating than regular trips to the kitchen at home for a cup of coffee. Ordering the day this way provides a new kind of freedom that seems most beneficial to one's bodily clock.

With this new ordering of the day, time is put to better use, and the word "pastime" begins to seem almost a profanation. Why should you want to pass time when it is so intrinsically valuable?

In my visits to a small monastery that keeps quite closely the hours and psalm cycles prescribed by St. Benedict, I found the morning hours to be particularly valuable. "Only an hour," one might think, "before I have to go over to the chapel for Lauds." But remarkable amounts of work can be done in that time. And instead of wasting the five minutes before the bell rings for the next Office, one writes a postcard to a friend or reads another page or two of a book. I have found myself being rather self-conscious about the way in which, back at home, with ten minutes before the start of a class, I stop by someone's office door for a chat. Not that there is anything wrong with friendly chats, but if one is simply passing time, the monastery day seems to be a judgment on the practice.

In the afternoon, the visitor may be out in the fields helping a couple of monks with a piece of heavy work. The group will probably not return to the chapel for None, the brief Office that divides the afternoon under the old-style *horarium*. Instead, reminding us of the once-familiar painting *The Angelus*, when the monastery bell sounds in the distance some fairly tattered books are pulled from a tool chest, and the Office is recited out in the fields. This makes particularly touching the phrase that concludes the final prayer of many of the hours: we ask the blessing of God upon ourselves "and on our absent brothers." Distance is of little importance; we pray for one another wherever we are.

We are, at the outset, disposed to think that it must be exceedingly tedious to use just one hundred and fifty psalms and a few additional hymns and canticles as one's lifetime prayers in common worship. The Master, on whose Rule St. Benedict modeled his own *Rule*, required that all his monks learn to read and that they learn all of the psalms by heart. One imagines that they soon enough became familiar. To the extent that they were known by heart, were they recited without attention?

I never carried out any experiment, but I became convinced that one could fire a cannon during the Office and the monks would not look up, though I am certain that, just as sleeping parents will hear their children crying, a person who falls ill during the Office and needs help would immediately be attended to. I became persuaded that one thing I could accomplish from being present at the Office was to learn more about concentration. Also, I began to take seriously the possibility of using the Book of Psalms for personal devotions. I wonder when, prior to this time, I had given careful thought to the words of psalms or hymns or prayers that are very familiar to me.

Whether one goes through them while visiting a monastery or just reads through them when time is available, one discovers that the psalms are a magnificent collection of prayers for all sorts of occasions. As C. S. Lewis shows in his book *Reflections on the Psalms*, they address all the con-

cerns of our lives, even to expressing the anger we sometimes feel toward others.

Specific psalms come to be associated with particular
times in the day. St. Benedict's distribution of the psalms
is exquisitely appropriate. The psalms with which the rising of the sun is greeted each morning at Lauds remind us
to praise the God of all creation. Read over Psalms 4, 90,
and 133, and judge whether there are any words better fitted
to putting one in a mood for repose through the night! These
particular psalms might be nice to teach our children. Young
children love familiar words—just make a mistake in reading one of their favorite stories! Also, the same psalms
would be quite a bit better for their elders than sleeping pills
or counting sheep.

Most of the people I have talked with in the guest house
confess to being ''night people,'' yet visitors who stay in
the monastery a few days readily adapt to the cycle as it
becomes increasingly comfortable. One is rising, more or
less, with the sun and going to bed, more or less, with the
sun. After a few days, it seems foolish that we ever permitted the invention of artificial light to move us to a cycle
so far removed from what is natural and benign. The monastic *horarium* is easily adapted to. When one returns from
a monastery, the body seems reluctant to return to the hours
we find convenient ''on the outside.''

If this seems odd, we might remind ourselves of the
hours farmers keep. Even more tellingly, they are the hours
we all tend to keep when, in what is surely a return to a
more natural cycle, we camp away from television and artificial light. That part of the *Rule* that seems most unlike
our own secular lives seems to point the way to a more
healthful schedule.

I have never been able to solve this problem to my own
satisfaction. On returning home, I soon go back to being
a night person all over again. If it didn't seem that getting
up early in the day would merely entail walking the dogs
earlier, I might try using the early hours of the day for some

undisturbed reading. Then I think about the absence (except for cats) of pets from the monastery.

Of course, we do not have a vocation to the religious life, and we have our own lives to lead. But when I realize this, I think of the prayers prayed in the fields. These prayers in the fields are among the most significant memories I carry with me. They particularly call to mind T. S. Eliot's marvelous phrase, "The lonely anchorite in his cell prays for the state of Christ's Church." People in religious life have been offering prayers throughout the hours of the day since the early days of the Church. And those of us not in religious life have sometimes regretted that there was not time for us to devote similar time to prayer and thought our lives spiritually deficient.

But, of course, we *are* the absent brothers and sisters of those who pray on our behalf throughout the days of their lives as monastics, and we *are* sharers of their prayers whether we think about it or not. Our busy lives would be similarly consecrated if we, even fleetingly throughout our day, thought that we heard a monastery bell calling us to prayer. They ring continuously on our behalf, too.

# VI

## PRAYER AND SILENCE

### Reading from the *Rule:* chapters 20, 42, 49, 52

Whenever we want to ask some favor of a powerful man, we do it humbly and respectfully, for fear of presumption. How much more important, then, to lay our petitions before the Lord God of all things with the utmost humility and sincere devotion (*RB* 20:1-2).

There may be no practice more difficult for us to understand than prayer. It is almost comical that when prayer in the schools is a topic of debate, much of what is being recommended as a prayer appropriate for use in schools is little more than the perfunctory recitation of an exceedingly noncommittal form of words or a quiet moment in which one reflects on a topic of one's choice—on God, if that is what one prefers. Whether the public school in America is an appropriate setting for authentic prayer is obviously a divisive legal issue, but the argument has less to do with the nature of prayer than with the history of our country and the nature of the public education system as it has recently developed.

Years ago Dennis Brogan defended the American public schools against their European critics, arguing that the public schools had created the nation. They continued inducting the children of immigrants into the great American experiment by introducing them to the traditions of the Founders, especially their—our?—shared values. It seems odd that today these same schools are the place where pluralism is most strenuously demanded. The present debate seems to ignore the question of whether education ought to be more than reading, writing, and computer programming, whether the nation is best served in this way.

Despite our indecision in these matters, I want to argue that the ritual aspect of prayer may provide a good start toward understanding prayer.

In numerous New Testament passages, Jesus is called "Rabbi." He is said by all to have been a great teacher. Thus it is noteworthy that the only time he is actually asked to teach anyone anything, his disciples ask him to teach them to pray. Perhaps even more instructively, he gives them a form of words to use. "When you pray, say. . . ."

At first, it might seem tedious praying the same prayers, the same psalms, over and over again. This seemed to me difficult to rebut until it occurred to me that my familiarity with breakfast has never caused me to be contemptuous of it. I also realize that, without having made any effort to memorize them, I can today sing the words of the hymns with which my public school days in England started, in the years before World War II.

Still, for reasons that are not altogether easy to explain, we have become a generation that attaches little significance to rote learning. In fact, rote learning is often cited as a horrible example of old-fashioned teaching. This trend was already beginning when my teachers were wont to say that it was less important to know facts than to know where they might be found. And since young people now can take calculators to school, learning the times tables seems quite unnecessary.

One has to wonder what will be in our heads in the long run if this continues. Simply catalogs of places to find things when we need them? Simply user's manuals for our personal computers? By this argument, students ought to have become much better at using the card catalog in the library—or its computerized substitute—than seems to be the case.

People who came back from Korean and Vietnamese prisoner-of-war camps told of the importance to them of what they had remembered from their youth. The times tables? Well, how about the rules for chess? And poetry and chapters from the Bible were most appreciated. American young people in the Peace Corps, incidentally, must often have wished their parents had obliged them to learn more things by heart. In countries like Korea, for example, social occasions typically require everyone present to recite some poetry or sing a song. As we have mentioned, as soon as the monks of the Master were literate they were set to learning to recite all the psalms.

No doubt it would be well if we all were capable of making coherent spontaneous prayers. Learning things by heart, especially prayers and psalms, would do much to improve the quality of our thinking when we attempt to be spontaneous.

In recent days, much has been heard around churches to the effect that prayers would be more meaningful if they were not the same prayers all the time. People who believe this are difficult to persuade otherwise. One wonders, however, if they ever notice how their minds are stimulated to wander when they come across unfamiliar phrases and jarring ideas in the order of worship. I recall a visiting minister who was a devotee of this view. In his prayers that morning, he said something like this: "We are grateful that you have taught us to love our enemies; we have not yet begun to love our friends." He must have said something else, preached a sermon even, but I spent all of the rest of the time wondering why he thought that was a good thing to say. I suspect that other people had the same experience.

Much has been written and even more has been

preached suggesting that the essence of prayer is some kind of appropriate mental and spiritual posture. Who would deny this? Certainly, insincerity would seem to invalidate any usefulness to praying. But we do have a problem when we accept the notion that emotion makes the difference between the genuine and the fake, the desirable and the undesirable. Thinking this, we have fallen into a trap. For example, it is often suggested—surely improperly—that, if one cannot be sincere in acting politely, it is better to be rude.

The greatest threat to sincerity in prayer is the disturbing thought that passes through our mind that we are not truly meaning what we are saying. With only the slightest encouragement, all of us can think of unworthy explanations of why we are doing some kind of useful act we had started to do in innocent goodness. In the same way, the greatest threat to concentration in prayer is the thought that we are not really concentrating. As we have said, monastics learn the habit of concentration.

For so many of us, it is simply impossible to know where to start. In his *Confessions*, St. Augustine says that before he was ready to receive baptism, he felt that he must solve all outstanding theological problems—the relation of God to time, for example. Before starting to pray must *I* solve all of these great problems and, on top of that, avoid distraction? I shall be a long time starting.

It is amazing how often these problems have been mentioned in the writings of the great souls of the Church from earlier centuries. Thus I was struck recently to find that remarkable woman of the turn of the fifteenth century, known only to history as Julian of Norwich, speaking to this very issue: ''[T]he prayer is profitable though you feel nothing, though you see nothing, yes, though you think you can do nothing. . . . He covets our continual prayer. . . . [T]his folly in our feelings is the cause of our weakness.''

It is interesting to note that chapter 20 of the *Rule*, while stressing that prayer should be sincere also asserts that it should be short. St. Benedict is talking here about private prayer during the saying of the Office in the abbey church.

It is important to regard the entire recitation of the psalms throughout the day as prayer. One says the psalms as the schedule calls for them, without regard to one's feelings at the moment. Our cultural "thing" for sincerity would suggest that we not say them unless we are "feeling" them. Not so.

In his marvelous *Screwtape Letters*, Lewis points out that a good strategy for the devil would be to insist that petitions can be genuine only if they are prayed with the proper concentration. The devil can then raise the interesting question of whether we are ever entirely concentrating while praying, so that, in the end, we never really pray. Lewis says—and surely he is correct—that when a person feels distracted, he or she must simply persist in praying. Thus, one develops the habit of allowing the *act* of praying to focus the mind rather than requiring the focus of our mind to make the prayer authentic. In this way, the experience of the recitation of the monastic Office can help the visitor understand prayer, even learn to pray.

When a visitor first joins in reciting the monastic Office, having newly "come in" and having left family and work behind, it is terribly difficult to put things out of mind. The newcomer—I am thinking of myself—finds himself noting where the various monks are seated and listening to see which of the monks' voices can be more readily heard; he wonders what is the front page story in today's newspaper and whether there might be a letter from his wife today. And on and on. It is easy to say, "I simply have to get myself in hand and stop this wandering of mind. Can't I bring myself to concentrate on anything?" It is a good question. As Lewis suggests, the attempt to concentrate is the best distraction ever invented.

So what must we do? We recite the Office hour by hour and find, as the hours and days pass, that our minds are increasingly bent to paying attention to the words until, fairly soon, we are actually praying through these words of the psalmist. Having reached this point, we feel that we might be ready to start praying on our own. Such lack of humility makes appropriate St. Benedict's words that such prayers "should always be brief."

What is useful about experiencing the monastic Office is the awareness that, despite one's wandering mind, the praying goes on, and we begin to understand that the Office is exemplary for us. I am being taught to let the praying go on even when I am beset by a wandering mind. Finally, my thoughts are brought back to the prayer and it is evidently my prayer and I feel that I am learning to pray.

For many of us, the problem with prayer is compounded by concerns over bodily attitudes. In earlier times, Presbyterian children in Scotland made fun of their Anglican neighbors because, in their services, the Anglicans were "doon on tha knees and opp agen." A little rhyme known to children had the Anglicans respond: "Presby, Presby, dinna bend; / Sit thee doon on mon's chief end."

For those of us raised in Christian denominations whose worship practices have been nonliturgical, it is difficult at first to feel comfortable bowing as part of praying, as monastics do. Of course, it would not matter if one did not bow, but one begins to do it out of politeness or to avoid the embarrassment of sticking out in a crowd—sparse though the crowd may be. And then, after a time, bowing begins to seem natural and proper and, finally, even desirable. With gesture in prayer, one realizes that the whole person is involved in worship. Worship is not simply a matter of thought and moral activity; it is an involvement of one's whole person. And this consideration leads one to thinking about the entire gestural life of the monastic: the embrace for the kiss of peace, so much more meaningful than the handshake, and so on.

As contrasted with Christian groups who have emphasized the individuality of belief and worship, Catholics have traditionally acknowledged that we do this act of worship together. Certainly there have been few things introduced into the worship of Christian churches that have caused more protests, more resentment, than acknowledging the presence of other folk by means of the kiss of peace, in whatever form that has been suggested. Many of us have been comfortable with the notion that what we do in church is essentially something that goes on in our heads. Bowing together and shaking hands says it is otherwise. Our religion, which includes our prayer, is something that involves the whole of us: mind, soul, and body. Prayer as well as more formal "religion" reminds us of our nature as social beings.

A complement to prayer of the monastery, and perhaps even harder to appreciate, is the silence. For most of us, silence is a negative good. It is a relief from the noise that permeates so much of life: the canned music in dentists' waiting rooms and department stores, the distant noise of airplanes even on the most peaceful summer days in the Smokies, the children's hi-fi late into the evening when we need to get some reading done.

The silence of a monastery is not, however, a merely negative good. It is a positive feature of daily life. Not simply the absence of the need to talk or be sociable, silence becomes the reflection of a positive attitude toward the self and even an affirmation of others. It is the manifestation of a reposeful spirit.

This may appear to be mere assertion. To experience the quiet of the monastery, however, is to discover that it is fact. We need to remember that, although the *Rule* speaks of the matter in a negative fashion—restraint of speech— the outcome is a positive quality both in the person and the community. Hence, "there are times when good words are to be left unsaid out of esteem for silence" (RB 6.2).

I am struck by the fact that one could conclude that a period of silence in public schools might be beneficial after all, and not merely as a kind of anonymous moment to be used as the individual sees fit. But again one comes to realize that the real significance of silence is the spiritual context in which it is found.

Finally, although the visitor may not immediately realize it, the dress of the monastic contributes to the quiet and peace. I have sometimes found it difficult to persuade monastics that their traditional garb has more significance than they might imagine—not least for their state of mind. Clearly, all who wear long skirts learn a certain grace in walking, and this, in turn, contributes to the quiet and peace of the monastery. Thus, dress is added to gesture as a reminder of the role of the body in a growing understanding of prayer.

Of course, we are but visitors to this community in which uniform dress of a rather medieval style is customary and proper. It is not *these* elements that we seek to imitate but the unity of spiritual activity and bodily life. We are not Christians by reason of a unique form of dress, though our manner of dress certainly affects the way we think of ourselves. Does our being Christian also affect the way we think of ourselves as well as the way we act toward other people?

Being Christian is itself a bodily act. We need to recall the words of the early Christian who taught that "the way we pray is the way we believe." Prayer, also, jibes with action.

Can we seriously entertain the thought that we might become more than we ever anticipated?

# VII

## DISCIPLINE

**Reading from the *Rule:* chapters 21–30, 41, 43–47, 50, 51, 63, 67, 68**

> It is the abbot's responsibility to have great concern and to act with all speed, discernment and diligence in order not to lose any of the sheep entrusted to him. He should realize that he has undertaken care of the sick, not tyranny over the healthy. . . . He is to imitate the loving example of the Good Shepherd who left the ninety-nine sheep in the mountains and went in search of the one sheep that had strayed (*RB* 27:5–8).

Chapters 22–30 of St. Benedict's *Rule* make us acutely aware that we live in a different century, as we read that "boys and the young, or those who cannot understand the seriousness of the penalty of excommunication, . . . should be subjected to severe fasts or checked with sharp strokes so that they may be healed" (*RB* 30.2–3). This seems unduly harsh, and I am reminded of George Orwell's description in *The Road to Wigan Pier* of the beatings he received as a schoolboy for failing to do well in Greek. In retrospect, he says, he is persuaded that beating a boy is a pretty good stimulus to his learning Greek.

There is no single topic that would cause us to comment on St. Benedict's understanding of human nature. Rather, that understanding is distributed throughout the entire *Rule*. There are constant indications that he recognizes our fallen-ness, which tradition has called original sin, as well as less profound but equally problematic tendencies to petty jealousy and just ordinary grumbling. We may think that St. Benedict is very severe in his discussion of discipline, but what he recommends in this regard is remarkably consistent with human dignity. And, he recognizes that superiors are just as prone to undesirable behavior.

St. Benedict's discussion of discipline is simpler and briefer than that in the Master's Rule. The principle is much the same—offenses against the community will bring some degree of exclusion from the common life of the community—but St. Benedict is free of the pettifoggery characteristic of the Master. The Master, for example, cannot imagine a guest going to the bathroom at night without a monk accompanying him to see that he doesn't steal some of the monastery's goods. In contrast, St. Benedict's direction concerning discipline displays both an understanding of human weakness and an affirmation of human integrity.

Initially, punishment is scarcely more than a fairly inconsequential form of exclusion from the monastic Office and from eating with the community. The degree of exclusion can become greater, but only under the most extreme circumstances is the individual actually expelled, and even then the person may be readmitted if repentant—several times!

The term "excommunication" is one that historians have managed to embroider to a remarkable degree; thus we have learned to speak of excommunication and burning at the stake in the same breath. In contrast with these extreme ideas, as some students recently reading the *Rule* with me noted, excommunication means, quite literally, being put out of the community *to some degree*. One might also reflect that the person doing the "putting out" is the offender, whose own act is, in effect, self-excommunicating. Yet in spite of this truth, people who have a tendency to break community are often quite vocal in their protests that they have done nothing of the kind, that it was not serious, that it was not their fault, and so on.

However warranted we might assume the action to be, we are made uncomfortable by the *Rule's* mention of punishment. Recalling scenes of Orwell's English classroom, we imagine children being caned or whipped for the mistakes they make. We simply do not know the degree to which there was physical punishment in accordance with the *Rule* during the time of St. Benedict. And while we may be disposed to dislike what we read there, the jury is surely out in the matter of whether our children are more effectively disciplined today, when physical punishment for misbehavior is largely excluded in public schools and, given the apparent increasing occurrence of child abuse, is increasingly suspect within the home.

Reading the *Rule* requires that we think soberly about the difference between discipline and punishment as it is typically conceived.

Punishment stems from the judgment that an unacceptable act has been committed and that the act warrants a penalty—perhaps largely to discourage others from following suit. What goes on in our prisons today, while undoubtedly punishment, is, for a great many of us, regarded as a means of reclaiming the individual into the society. Although the death penalty can be nothing other than punishment, the absurdly long sentences sometimes handed down in lieu of a death sentence imply that after some time, perhaps a very long time, the individual will be considered for release. It is punishment in fact but discipline in theory.

We do well to remember that discipline, which often seems virtually indistinguishable from punishment (and sometimes in the *Rule* is called punishment), is actually a form of teaching. Subjects in universities are identified as disciplines. Until the person has finally shown that he/she is beyond reconciliation with the monastic community, he/she is disciplined in order that he/she may be reclaimed.

Despite the apparent harshness of the penalties suggested in the *Rule,* St. Benedict is remarkably sensitive to the needs of both the individual and the community. He understands that the community is significantly injured if a member's misbehavior goes unchecked, but he does not immediately lower the boom on those who fail in their responsibilities to their brothers or sisters. It has to be determined whether the individual understands the matter of concern and its consequences. When discipline is necessary, there is first a parental kind of reproof followed by increasingly severe attempts to encourage the individual to reform.

We should like to ask some questions. Chapter 28 suggests that when all else has failed the community should pray for the reconciliation of the errant one. This would seem to some of us a leaving to last what might have been first. Perhaps the elements of discipline coming first were, at that time, regarded as relatively inconsequential. Being caned in an English classroom hurt quite a bit, but one was not marked for life. Being named—even in prayer, perhaps particularly in prayer—as a person close to a final divorce from the community could be an even more serious matter of concern for the individual.

St. Benedict does not find it necessary to provide a justification for a ready punishment at what may seem to be the merest offense, nor does he think the community need not be considered where misconduct is concerned. Punishment is administered for the purpose of reconciling the individual with the community, not simply for the sake of punishing.

We err in both directions in our lives. Especially with individuals we love, we tend to be indulgent to an extreme that many cultures would find incomprehensible, always hoping that faults will be remedied. We know that bad behavior unchecked inevitably escalates, but we tend to do little to bring about a change. Then, when hope for spontaneous amendment is lost, we concentrate on punishment. Our despair over the constant failure of this process is revealed when our only solution is yet more draconian punishment.

As we reflect on the *Rule,* we seem to hear St. Benedict suggesting that love must be tougher than we are accustomed to making it. Individuals ought to be brought to recognize their responsibilities to the community at an early age, but the community can never lose sight of its responsibilities to and for the individuals. It is not a simple choice between acceptance and rejection. Acceptance into the community must imply a willingness for the wise use of sanctions. Even when individuals must be separated from the community, the fact of their belonging must not—cannot—be forgotten.

In general, we have fallen into thinking of excommunication as a one-time thing. It is never this for St. Benedict. We are accustomed to thinking that Geneva under Calvin was the strictest community known in relatively recent times. Even in Calvin's Geneva the city records show that individuals were excommunicated numbers of times. Clearly, as with St. Benedict, there was the constant concern to reconcile the individual if at all possible. We imagine the situation entirely focused upon the erring person, but is excommunication anything other than an affirmation of the community and its desire to make us better than we might otherwise be?

In earlier days it was common practice in daily chapter meetings—the chapter of faults as it was sometimes called—for individuals to accuse others of faults against the community. Humility required that accusations be silently accepted by the persons accused. This says something about the nature of humility, but principally it signifies that love must be sufficiently strong to take to task even those whom we particularly love because we love them. We tend too readily to accept the breaking of relationship. In our day, most separations from community come from the individuals themselves; few communities are sufficiently confident of their own significance to use separation as a means of discipline. How much better our society might be if we were to take with utter seriousness the promises we make to one another, and if both parents and children were to recognize that the bonds they have with one another can never be wholly severed. "For better or worse" the marriage vows say, and the monastic's vow of stability is the counterpart of those promises. The *Rule* emphasizes that relationships once formed can never be wholly erased, nor can the need for discipline be overlooked.

In connection with the monastic's vow of stability is a phrase which has puzzled scholars but which is important here. We are told that the Latin of the phrase *conversatione morum suorum* is itself strange. This is typically called "conversion of life" and, together with stability and obedience, constitutes the promise to live the monastic life as prescribed by the *Rule*. Difficult as this phrase is, it has come to mean for Benedictines the cultivation of a life proper to their vocation as monastics. One is reminded of the beautiful phrase from the wedding service of the *Anglican Book of Common Prayer:* the petition that the newly married may be given a state of mind "fit for their new estate." Many of our contemporaries would find it strange to suggest that one might enter into a relationship acknowledging that his or her personality should need to be changed to fit this new style of life. But that is what the *Rule* clearly requires of the member of the community.

A term much used in Catholic circles in the past was "formation." Consistent with the practices in the Church described by this term was the assumption that the organizations we joined had appropriate responsibility for forming our character. Nowadays, however, we have made it difficult to think seriously about this possibility by allowing the term "indoctrination" to hold only bad connotations. Thus, we see our social organizations as the sum of the personalities who make them up. By contrast, the *Rule of St. Benedict* suggests that we think of conforming our attitudes to the communities to which we have promised ourselves. It is a form of discipline that, doubtless, many of our contemporaries would find repugnant in the extreme.

Recent social attitudes do indeed seem to emphasize retaining a way out of commitments without personal cost. The attitude becomes self-fulfilling: all commitments become tentative and lose any lasting significance. One wonders whether this unwillingness to make lasting commitments to the important institutions of our lives is not at the root of our sense of ourselves as a people who lack the benefits of discipline. That people desire to have a way to get out of commitments is typically defended in the name of freedom. On reflection, however, we might see that this is an example of the trivialization of the understanding of freedom that characterizes our modern age.

I am struck by the fact that the men of a wedding party waiting to enter the church often joke with the groom about this being his last opportunity to avoid giving up his freedom. Obviously, at such an hour, a minister can do little more than smile faintly when hearing this, but I have always wanted to give these young men a lecture. What seems perfectly clear is that we have totally failed to recognize that new relationships provide opportunities for new kinds of freedom.

Our whole culture has been bogged down with the philosopher Hobbes's notion that the exemplary and free human being is the isolated creature, the creature who gives up this freedom and that for the sake of safety or convenience. Biologists would recognize that the isolated creature is hardly to be called a creature. By itself, it would die without reproducing its kind. Surely that is not the basic understanding we should have of freedom.

This misunderstanding of freedom fails to grasp the fact that life is always lived in context. A good definition of freedom, I believe, would show it to be characteristic of persons willingly identifying themselves in and through the context of their lives. St. Paul is free when he says, ''I have learned, in whatsoe'er estate I am, therewith to be content.'' Freedom is the desire to affirm myself and to identify myself through the choices I have made. It is trivial to suggest that a married person is no longer free to live as a single person. By the same token, the unmarried person is not yet free to live as a married person.

The person who, having made a commitment, wishes to be free of it is not really desiring freedom so much as expressing the childish desire to be able to live life over. Perhaps one or other of the partners was incapable of living up to what the commitment required. That the relationship will be ended should not be confused with a return to the previous condition.

An ordered life, a disciplined life, is not lived at the price of freedom. One might even hold that freedom is enhanced as the relationships in which I find myself are enriched. That would explain how we might be persuaded that our greatest freedom is found in our relationship with God.

Perhaps we shall not know how to deal with one another lovingly until we accept the principle that promises to one another are never to be broken because the breaking of commitments attacks the possibility of being free. It is the intentional permanence of monastic vows and the ready acceptance of all that such permanence entails that makes the discipline of the community credible and its members free.

One of St. Benedict's most notable insights in this whole matter of being human in community lies in his understanding of the role of the seemingly inconsequential. We quite readily distinguish between the important and the unimportant aspects of life together. It seems to us that humming at the dinner table (I wonder if I still *do* that) and failure to remember to deposit checks in our account are relatively distinguishable: one seems unimportant, the other important. St. Benedict, however, seems to be very severe about what we probably think of as inconsequential. Grumbling about this or that because the decision made was not what we had desired, he says, is simply unacceptable. My commitment to a relationship is not honored if I know there are little things I do that tend to undermine it. We have taught ourselves to say, well, they are only little things, but, as the writer of the *Song of Songs* reminds us, it is the little foxes that spoil the vineyards when they are in flower.

One of the little things that can be irritating is mentioned in chapter 48. St. Benedict, talking about the summertime permission of monks to rest on their beds after Sext, says, "Should a brother wish to read privately, let him do so, but without disturbing the others." Offhand, I should not have seen how it was possible that a reader could disturb others, but Dom Jean LeClercq points out that, at the time, "reading" was still reading aloud. Then we discover that St. Augustine was surprised when visiting St. Ambrose that he was reading without voicing the words.

A colleague of mine has often joked about people who can't read without moving their lips. The joke really goes into reverse because the speaking aloud was a means of underlining the text as it was being read. There! For many of us, marking the text is simply an alternative to the older practice of reading aloud.

Here, as with prayer, we discover the wisdom of these ancient folk: we really do not take a reading to heart until we have somehow embodied it.

A visitor today would hardly be cognizant of any discipline that might be in effect, but I did hear a conversation that exemplifies what I think of as discipline in relation to community spirit. I was working out in the fields with a young candidate and a quite senior monk. Perhaps because of my presence, we talked sporadically through the afternoon, and then, in a spirit of friendliness, the young man said that he was very much looking forward to the following day. He was going to be the one who took the weekly trip into the nearby town for necessary purchases, and since he was going to miss lunch, he was looking forward to having a great big hamburger. One of my students later commented that the young man was suffering the pangs of a "Big Mac attack."

"Why will you be doing this?" asked the older monk.

"Well, because I'll miss dinner (the noon meal)."

"Why must you miss lunch?"

"Well, because I'll be going in at eleven-thirty."

"Couldn't you leave after we have eaten?"

"Well . . ."

I felt quite sorry for him and wanted to say, "Oh, why don't you just let him go?" But, of course, the older monk was pointing to the significance of excommunication: one does not eat with the brothers. I never talked with the older monk about the incident, but I assume he would have said that a candidate for the community needs to see his actions in relation to what the *Rule* has to say.

It looked like punishment, but I see that it was discipline, and I hope that I might have had the grace, had the situation been mine, to be either teacher or apt student.

# VIII

## COMMITMENT

### Reading from the *Rule:* chapters 53, 58–61

Let him be told: "This is the law under which you are choosing to serve. If you can keep it, come in. If not, feel free to leave" (*RB* 58:10).

**B**eing a nation of joiners, we Americans are usually ready to welcome virtually anyone into our clubs and associations. No wallet could hold the card of every organization to which we belong. In addition to the numerous credit cards, there would be cards for fraternal organizations, for various community groups, for political clubs and pressure groups.

A visitor to the planet would surely think it strange that the most intimate and socially most important of relationships appears at the lower end of the scale: one can get married with less effort than it takes to join many of these organizations. The higher degrees in Masonic lodges, for example, require long periods of candidacy. I have been irritated over the years, when attempting to set a time for a church group meeting, to be told that such-and-such a night is out of the question because the lodge meets that night. I wanted to ask which was more important. But I have come to realize that I was, in fact, being told what was more important to that person. I wondered whether, if it took several years to achieve full membership in the Christian congregation, membership in the Church would rank higher among the groups laying claim to our loyalty.

One can develop a distinct sense of déjà vu when thinking of these matters. We read of long periods of initiation in the early days of the Church, and we marvel at the incredible fact that people who had been disciplined for some sin would sometimes spend years seeking to be fully readmitted to communion. Some have a sense that a more rigorous discipline would be beneficial to the overall meaningfulness of Church membership, but others of us feel that the Church is in such a marginal situation today—surrounded as it is by all manner of apparently attractive religious bodies—that it would be dangerous to attempt to require more of communicants. Given that we hear the pros and cons of such matters being argued both in the Church and in the media, it is instructive to read what St. Benedict has to say about joining the monastery.

Although visitors should be cordially welcomed, St. Benedict requires that they not be encouraged too readily to think of becoming members of the monastic community. This is not done on the principle that immediately occurs to me: should I want such a person belonging to one of my groups? Nor is it, perhaps, what Groucho Marx once said. Evidencing an acute understanding of the Christian awareness of personal sinfulness, he commented, ''I shouldn't want to join any club that would have me as a member.'' Rather, St. Benedict's concern is that the candidate fully understand the implications of the monastic life: on three formal occasions the *Rule* is read to the candidate from beginning to end.

St. Benedict's remarkable caution in this regard would be regarded as downright strange by many of our contemporaries. We so often hear that persons should be free to walk away from relationships that have become boring or burdensome. Some relationships, of course, have legal entailments, but even these ought not to be pressed if individuals no longer value the relationships. According to this kind of thinking, if there is no apparent sanction against leaving a monastery, why is it important to be so deliberate about joining? The candidate for membership will have spent several years in study and work and will have made some good friends, no doubt, even if one is supposed to have the same kind of relationship with every member of the community. And now, if the person thinks there is something that might be better than joining the community, let that be done. That seems possible under the *Rule*. No one is prevented from leaving the monastery if determined to do so. Why, then, should it be made so difficult to become a member of the community?

Here is the crux of the matter. In the opinion of many, we should be free to dissolve relationships at will. Thus we should be free to enter relationships just as readily. Why not?

The question can only be answered, I believe, by recognizing that St. Benedict meant to swim against the tide of allowing casual promises. The person who puts a value on genuine relationships also needs to do this. To enter the monastic community a person must seriously intend what he or she promises those who will become his brothers or sisters—and they also what they promise by accepting him. Promises should be taken with such deliberation that one cannot imagine abrogating them later. This would seem to have been in St. Benedict's mind.

There are two considerations that make it difficult for even the most trivially minded to think of revoking the promises made by the Benedictine monastic. The first of these is pragmatic and has to do with property.

The *Rule* proposes a concrete element that makes the vows to the monastic community more sobering than the marriage vows, which are, for most of us, their closest analogy. This is the requirement concerning property. Nothing like an antenuptial agreement is possible here. As the marriage service used to say, "With all my worldly goods, I thee endow." Individuals enter the monastic community without anything of their own. All possessions must either be disposed of before coming to the monastery to take initial vows or given to the monastery on entering. If one were subsequently to leave—and this condition is common both to St. Benedict's *Rule* and that of the Master—the person would take nothing but the clothing worn on entering.

The solemn intent of this provision is underlined in the case of boys being "given" to the monastery. If the child of a rich family enters the monastery, it is required that he be formally and legally disinherited by his parents. There must be nothing like a "blind trust" that he could later lay claim to.

One enters the monastery, so to speak, naked and owning nothing. Under these circumstances, promises would seem to be altogether serious and binding. But while the considerations from these practical elements are sobering, they are not categorical. People often have experienced penury and preferred it to continuing in a situation they no longer desired. The individual must judge. This is a prudential consideration weighing against leaving. The other consideration mentioned by St. Benedict is of no economic significance. Its weight is solely moral, social, and religious.

The second consideration that makes it difficult to think of leaving the monastery is a particular vow among what *RB 1980: The Rule of St. Benedict* calls "the Benedictine vows": stability, *conversatione morum suorum* (mentioned in ch. VII), and obedience. Poverty and chastity, along with obedience, make up the "evangelical counsels," which are not mentioned in the *Rule* but are obviously assumed.

At the time he takes his solemn vows after a long period of testing, the monk offers the vow of stability, promising that he will live with these men in this monastery to the end of his days. Forever after they will consider him their *frater*. If this is so, can he readily disavow his promise? The solemn vows of sisters are entirely comparable and require identical consideration.

In the opening chapter of the *Rule,* St. Benedict denies that one can really be a monk and wander from monastery to monastery, as was common in his day. One can imagine our own contemporaries making an argument for a community that is easy to enter and easy to leave, but St. Benedict wanted to remedy the abuses that had infected the monasticism of his time, and so he calls for stability. If one is to promise stability and take the matter of making promises seriously, then it is not desirable that they be too readily made. The promise of stability is especially sobering. St. Benedict raises the question for us: is genuine community possible without such sober and binding promises? In a day when marriage might be interpreted as a state of serial monogamy, the notion of dwelling in a lifelong relationship is in many quarters rarely encountered.

It seems reasonable in our time that a person breaking off a relationship like marriage would say something like, "I don't love her any more." We are so accustomed to hearing this kind of remark that it does not strike us as peculiar. But some reflection would show that the person is commenting on an emotional condition as if it were like a condition of the heart or lungs. It would be difficult to find comments like this from centuries before our own.

A saying of our Lord which makes for jokes from time to time is, "A man who has lusted after a woman in his heart has committed adultery with her already." Surely our Lord did not mean that a vagrant thought passing through one's head is tantamount to the act it stands for. That would lead to the most incredible moral confusion imaginable—the kind of moral confusion ascribed to President Carter as a result of his famous interview in *Playboy* magazine. What our Lord is pointing to is not the passing thought but the entertainment and cultivation of the thought. Not to resist the thought is to will the sin, if not the act. The *Rule,* in its talk about humility, points us in the right direction—we should attempt to discipline our minds in the same way that we exercise our bodies.

So it would be the case that our moral commitments should be the schoolteacher of our emotions. Our lives should not be the feckless consequence of emotions. The hope of our society to overcome the curse of racism is meaningless unless we are able to school our emotions. They are not the immovable foundations of our morality.

It would be appropriate to say to people undertaking a lifelong commitment that they are now responsible for cultivating states of mind consistent with that commitment. Rather than thinking of ourselves as if our life were a theater of our emotions, we should do well to be instructed by St. Thomas in thinking about marriage in terms of a life of friendship.

It is clear that St. Benedict desires the would-be monastic to transcend any romantic fascination with the idea of becoming a member of the monastic community. The commitment needs to be founded on something beyond a passing emotion. It is clear from what St. Benedict says about having candidates for admission to the monastic community stand knocking at the door and so on—and not least what he says about their having the entire *Rule* read to them on several occasions—that he wants vows to be seriously considered and taken only after proper consideration.

The vows most seriously undertaken by most of us are those of marriage. Marriage vows differ from those of the monastic in one vital respect. The monastic's vows have admitted the person to membership in an ongoing community, whereas marriage vows create a community where none existed before. For a long time before a candidate is permitted to take vows, he or she participates in the life of the monastic community, experiencing its discipline as well as all its other aspects. The candidate is free to leave at any time during this period.

Because candidates are free to leave at any time, they cannot really know what the permanent monastic life is like.

But the men or women among whom the candidates live are themselves bound by those promises, and what the candidate comes to know of their relationship allows him or her to judge the nature of the community. Marriage is different. Before the two individuals make their promises to each other, there is no marriage, no married community. One observes the marriage of one's parents and the marriages of one's friends, but the individual experience of the commitment to marriage is profound and virtually incomparable. Trial marriages would seem to provide evidence of a sort, but, sadly for those who have advocated the idea, trial marriages provide evidence only of a relationship that is devoid of the essence of marriage: commitment. Couples who live together "without benefit of clergy," as that condition was once characterized, are simply that: people living together. Clearly, sexual experience is not the experience of marriage. For these couples, there is as yet no marriage to experience.

Various well-meaning individuals have suggested trial marriages or conditional marriage vows: not "so long as we both shall live" but "so long as our love shall last," for example. It is difficult to know what commitment is expressed in such words, and the Christian community can only reject the notion of trial marriage as foolish on the face of it. What distinguishes marriage from all other relationships between men and women begins with the promises they make to each other. Many will testify that their marriage did not really become real to them until, after despairing of finding fulfillment in the relationship, they realized that it was a relationship for life and began to work to make it so.

What might be learned from the *Rule* in this instance, then, is the insistence that vows not be lightly made. On the theory that people ought to be free to leave whenever they desire, there is no reason to expect that one's partner in a relationship will respond to a desire to make the relationship permanent. By analogy to the monastic life, however, entering marriage should be a matter of long reflection; the intention of entering the relationship should be in principle irrevocable.

There is another aspect of this uniqueness of marriage that makes it dissimilar to the monastic life. It is what is conveyed by the scriptural notion that a married couple become one flesh. Although those in a state of marriage experience community, it is a community unique to the couple. Even here, however, St. Benedict may have had an insight that is pertinent to and confirms our non-monastic promises in marriage. The vow of stability inhibits the practice that was common in the early days of monasticism: the practice of individuals to live at will first with one group and then with another.

As chapter 61 of the *Rule* indicates, St. Benedict did not rule out the possibility that a monk who has started his life with one community might be accepted into another. His comments in this connection indicate that the abbot must carefully determine that this is not a monk who casually shops his loyalties around. There is sad evidence that people who are casual in the forming of sexual relationships discover that they are unsure that anything other than casual relationships are possible in this life. In his recent and influential *Closing of the American Mind*, Alan Bloom comments on his observation that the sexual freedom in which the students he observes grew up makes it exceedingly difficult for them to take seriously the possibility of a monogamous commitment. They lack, he feels, the sense of a discovered uniqueness in a relationship with this one person of the opposite sex, and the commitment of authentic marriage is thus difficult for them to envisage. That many of them are the products of broken marriages adds to this tendency. As Bloom comments, there is real sadness in the commonness of broken marriage. The children of such marriages, and many children who observe them, have no sense that they are in the one human relationship—that of child to parents—that once would have been regarded as ineradicable. That children's relationships with parents are broken injures their sense of the possibility of commitment.

The vow of stability, the indissolubility of marriage. Perhaps married folk and monastics have interesting things to talk about. Their commitment to God as the Lord of human life is the profound source of what they have in common.

# IX

## POSSESSING AND USING

**Reading from the *Rule:* chapters 33, 34, 39, 40, 54, 55**

Nothing is so inconsistent with the life of any Christian as overindulgence (*RB* 39:8).

One can have interesting conversations with monastics about the principles of chapters 33 and 34 of the *Rule:* that the monk shall own nothing but shall be afforded use of articles he needs.

Particularly if they entered the monastery at an early age and some time ago, monastics are inclined to think that lay-persons have an intense pride in their possessions, compared with monastics who have no possessions to be proud of. Yet there are some who use nice fountain pens (I like fountain pens, so I notice), have available all of the books they need, use a radio (at appropriate times to be sure), and so on. In many ways, monastics of all but the most severe monasteries have the use of much that their counterparts outside of the monastery might own. Most are not lacking the use of the kinds of things that persons in secular life would think necessary or even desirable.

Because monastics are aware that they do not own things, it seems to them significant that people outside the monastery *do* own things. It is hard for them to imagine that laypeople might be largely oblivious to the fact of ownership. Surely it must be the case that lots of people live in houses and use television sets and cars without, more than once in a blue moon, remarking to themselves that these are *their* houses, *their* television sets, and so on. We forget what happiness we got from owning our first car. I was reminded of this by a member of my Sunday School class who, reading what was just written, said that she got an immense thrill out of her first car—which she did not buy until after she had finished law school just a year or two earlier.

But we do forget, so that, later, much of what we own we regard more as conveniences than anything else. Of my house, on which I did huge amounts of work when we had just bought it, I wonder sometimes if any of our children might want to use it. I hope that whoever does later own it may appreciate it for its very sound construction and the good work I did on it. In fact, I feel about the house much as I feel about a favorite vista in the Smokies. It ought to be appreciated for its fine qualities. Is it, perhaps, characteristic of young people to have great pride of ownership that diminishes as they grow older?

But whether we take great pride in our possessions or think little about them, all of us would be significantly enlightened if we came to think of possessions essentially as things of which we have more or less continuing use. The principle is a good one: we should not make fetishes of the things we possess. Further, drawing an appropriate relationship between monastic and secular life, we should not seek to possess things for which we do not have a continuing and appropriate use.

Although expressed in terms of ownership and nonownership, the principle is essentially one of stewardship and the capacity for generosity. As we become aware of the growing horror that stems from our thoughtless use of natural resources, we might well express this principle not only by care in the use of resources commonly said to be scarce—fuel and food—but also by careful consideration of *all* the things we use. Why should we need reminders from the government or the Sierra club or the total on a fuel bill to make us think of being careful stewards of the earth's resources? How much better to be careful with all the things we need and use and simply not hold on to the things we do not need. As I hike in the Pisgah National Forest near Asheville, North Carolina, I wonder how much greater was Commodore Vanderbilt's pleasure because he owned what I now enjoy. I feel grateful that the U.S. Forest Service saves me from finding fences and locked gates surrounding these marvelous areas, but I can't think that ownership could add anything to my experience of them.

Although the *Rule of St. Benedict* says nothing of the matter in this context, our stewardship of our world's natural resources and the resources of our families makes it possible for us to consider the needs of others.

A good deal of nonsense has been written concerning the control over nature given to Adam as spoken of in Genesis. This has been construed as an invitation—principally heard, it strangely seems, by Christians rather than Hebrews—to use natural resources as if they might never be diminished. In rebuttal, Rene Dubos has noted that Lynn White and others have spoken extravagantly of St. Francis as the saint for the ecology-minded. This seems to stem from St. Francis's expressed concern for animals and his admiration of nature in general. Dubos points out, however, that the Benedictines have actually been the ecologists over the centuries.

What the *Rule's* teaching about ownership implies is not some trendy practice of ecological principles. Like the Scriptures, the *Rule* calls us to live in the world while acknowledging it to be God's world and accordingly showing proper concern for our brothers and sisters and for all aspects of creation. Categorically put, it is not the mere ability to purchase things that gives us the moral right to own them. It would be desirable to follow the great saints of the Christian tradition in living somewhat simpler lives regardless of financial status. Then, no doubt, we should be moved to give proper thought to our stewardship of financial resources.

Of course, monastics will always tend to live simpler lives than most of us find desirable. But the *Rule* is not niggardly. One is to have what one has need of, so long as it can be provided.

To live in this fashion would raise significant questions about our relationship to the needy in our society and to institutions that exist to serve the needs of our citizens. Is it possible that by thinking in terms of use rather than of possession the entire Christian community, through its parishes and churches, could once more become the model of care and concern for the human community? Perhaps this kind of effort is beginning to be common and to be socially significant.

At the moment, our society is alarmed because welfare and medical costs seem to be outrunning our capacity to provide for the needs of our citizens. Do we recall that hospitals were originally not public or proprietary but institutions of the Church? And that the Christian community felt a particular responsibility for the genuinely needy in its midst? Is it possible that private charity might begin to reduce our reliance on the impersonal social services of our government? At first blush, it seems unlikely that the churches could make a dent in the problem. But President Reagan once pointed to a striking statistic with respect to unemployment: if every employer, large and small, were able to hire one additional worker, the unemployment problem would disappear. Of course, this is not the way in which Detroit's unemployment will be solved. It is, however, a way of illustrating the miracle of the feeding of the five thousand: a little boy's lunch made the difference.

One of the most interesting—and perhaps hotly debatable—articles in the Benedictine sesquimillenial pub-

lication *RB 1980: The Rule of St. Benedict* may be that which
suggests that the earliest exemplars of monasticism may not
have been the heroic fathers living their days in barren
deserts but rather the Christian couple who, after their children were of a sufficient age, continued to live together but
now as celibates, dedicating their lives to the service of the
Christian community. If this theory is correct, then it was
only somewhat later that monasticism was identified with
desert dwellers or with communities segregated by sex and
living in out of the way places.

In the early Church, many Christian couples lived ascetic
lives, dedicating themselves to the service of the Christian
community. Reflecting on the lives of these Christians raises
interesting questions about the relevance of St. Benedict's
*Rule* for all Christians. Of course, we are not going to join
monasteries in large numbers, but perhaps we might undertake to live the lives of dedication that marked these lay
members of the early Christian Church. This might be the
revivification of the Church for which many of us pray.

One of the results of thinking along these lines might
be a renewal of interest in the monastic invention of oblates attached to particular monastic communities. The term
comes from the offering of oneself to God. A renewal of
monastic oblates might be the beginning of a genuine transformation, through which we might come to think about
the nature of the Christian life as a life of action in the world.
If the authors of *RB 1980* are correct in their thesis, perhaps
enquirers about the *Rule's* possibilities—ourselves?—could
be the first wave of a revival of monasticism in the world.

Along these lines, a friend of mine who is single took
early retirement from professional employment and sought
entry into the life of a Benedictine house. Of course, monastic communities are aware of the responsibilities they have
for their members who are growing old, and no vital community could commit itself to becoming, in effect, a retirement home. Yet God may call us to vocations at times other
than those that have seemed the standard. What might be

the consequence of numbers of us dedicating our mature years and our retirement incomes to the relief of society's needy? We live as people who need to try to make certain of our future, as if ownership of property or of pension rights will give us that assurance. Yet we hear the Gospel preached: does not our Father know what we have need of?

It would be impossible for most of us to take the psychologically threatening step of simply trusting in God to supply our needs. Those of us who are responsible for families would be loath to cast aside the prudential provisions we have made to guard against the unforseen needs of the future. What would be the consequences for our daily life and for our communities if we started thinking about using our goods instead of possessing them?

In *After Virtue*, Alasdair MacIntyre, after demonstrating the fractured nature of our present-day society, concludes that what might reclaim our society to a morally coherent condition would be for us to experience the renewal that Europe derived from the monasteries of St. Benedict during the medieval period. Perhaps he is merely citing a cultural phenomenon that he would wish the West to witness again. But those who read and think about St. Benedict will consider MacIntyre to be a possible prophet.

# X

## SERVICE

**Reading from the *Rule:* chapters 35–38, 48, 53, 57**

The brothers should serve each other *(RB* 35:1).

Great care and concern are to be shown in receiving poor people and pilgrims, because in them more particularly Christ is received; our very awe of the rich guarantees them special respect *(RB* 53:15).

On the first visit to a small monastery, few things are quite so bothersome as the way one is served by the monastics. There is no other word. I shall never forget how much it bothered me when an older monk brought food to my place, returning after a time to see whether I had had enough. It seemed inappropriate that such a venerable person should be serving me. Of course, it was not my home, but I wanted in the worst way to insist that he sit down and that I serve him. I wondered what might happen if some entirely arrogant individuals were to come to the monastery. Would they not find it unnerving to be served so readily and without any indication of reserve? The moral force of what might have appeared to be complete passivity suddenly seems credible. How can one resist such complete willingness to serve?

I also found myself wondering how I might ever be able to serve the monks, whether I was worthy even to seek to be of service. It struck me that never before could I have framed the thought in quite such a way—to be worthy to serve. Cardinal Newman's lovely description of a gentleman fits the monk rather well: "He makes light of favours while he does them, and seems to be receiving when he is conferring." It is difficult to believe that many in this ordinary secular life have ever considered it a privilege to serve others. It is the kind of thought that comes to mind when one visits monasteries.

To some extent, the whole matter goes back to the character of the monastic, which is accomplished through living the *Rule of St. Benedict.* It is compatible with the humility of the monastic ideal that one have this kind of relationship with other persons, particularly others within the monastic community. I should like to propose that the ideal of service, which has to do with one's whole character formation, is a matter worthy of special consideration.

The entirely remarkable nature of service as an ideal is that it removes calculation from our relationship with other human beings. We have only to think of the misery we feel when we have been afforded something less than splendid service in a restaurant and come at last to pay the bill. It seems that the matter should not go ignored and unmentioned. Does one leave a card commenting that the service was appalling? Does one leave a minuscule tip as a symbolic message? Does one think that perhaps the waiter has had a particularly rugged day and that, in any event, there may have been problems at home?

In situations like this, most of us have probably insisted—at least to ourselves—that it is degrading to make individuals dependent on tips for their income. How much better it would be, we think, if there were proper wages for service in a restaurant and no additions were called for. We cannot imagine overturning the established order in such matters. But in these reflections we rethink the prin-

ciple proposed by the *Rule:* that our service to others ought
to be the cheerful duty that we owe them.

In a monastery, this ideal may be close to being realized.
After all, in a monastery everyone does one's share of the
work, and turnabout is fair play. That doesn't quite obtain
in the matter of guests, although guests are often invited
to do a share of the work—which seems like a privilege.
I felt that I had graduated when I was invited—invited!—
to help wash the pans after dinner. In any event, guests
are guests of the entire community, and so the monastic
serves his brothers or sisters in serving his brothers' or sisters' guests. At least, one can imagine the argument going
that way.

Within the family, something of a similar nature could
be imagined. Unfortunately, relationships within the family have been injured considerably by the commercial way
in which our contributions one to the other have been interpreted in recent literature. While there are a great many
people who are little respected for the necessary work they
do, current notions of self-worth invite even quite privileged
people to consider themselves put upon when requested
to assist another person. This leads to a calculating understanding of the individual's role both in the family and in
all other relationships.

We need to be sensible about the rights of individuals
in relationships. As the principal case in point, there is no
reason for one person—unfortunately usually the mother—
to do all of a family's domestic work. That this was never
justifiable, however, was not because the cheerful service
of others is not good. There is a perfectly pragmatic reason
why domestic work should not fall entirely to the mother
but should be shared among other members of the household: it is part of learning what it is to be a member of a
community. Newspapers have recently been commenting
on the problems now seen in one-child families in China.
The problems of being an only child in our own society have
perhaps been exaggerated, but what about children brought

up in a society formally dedicated to the one-child family? Each of the children grows up as the sole concern of two parents and four grandparents, and without having learned how to deal with siblings. For that matter, think of whole generations of children growing up without knowing the rather special relationships that often exist between a child and uncles and aunts. What must be the situation of a child who has never learned that there are other members of the household who must be regarded as worthy of attention?

The *Rule* suggests an overarching reason for requiring a significant amount of shared work around the family dwelling. It is not that service is degrading and, therefore, ought to be spread around. Such thinking is immoral. Nor is pragmatism a final criterion—learning how to take care of ourselves as children so that we can manage when we no longer live in our parents' home. It is simply that we ought to be learning to be of service to one another. This is the monastic principle: that we learn to serve one another and take satisfaction in affording that service.

One of the smallest rites in the oratory is that in which the week's servers and readers offer thanks for the assistance they have received from God during the week, and those who are about to serve ask for assistance in the coming week. It might seem to be like the family passing a resolution of appreciation for the person who has washed the week's dishes. And why not? Washing the dishes is not just something to be done. It is done for the sake of the members of the household.

Each family works out details in ways appropriate to its own members. Some families will find specialization of responsibilities acceptable. Others will want all members to participate in the varied chores of the household, so that if fathers participate in the ordinary aspects of child care (as many did before it was so much talked about), so much the better for everyone. And so on.

Talk about service becomes most pointed, of course, when payment is involved. If cheerful service is the ideal, what about the significant salary differentials that exist in our society? The larger salaries peculiarly go to those whose work tends to be intrinsically interesting, even intrinsically rewarding. Those whose work is—or would be—most readily missed tend to be relatively poorly paid. I think of garbage collectors. The people who hold highly skilled jobs or jobs that require extended education have put in years of preparation before their work can be rewarded. Of course. But the years of preparation were rarely years of drudgery, and most of us who underwent extended education were substantially supported by the benevolence of predecessors and by the taxes of state and national government.

There are two considerations which grow out of our reflection on the *Rule:* the ethics of personal wealth and the ideal of a profession. We have mentioned the first of these in chapter IX. Here we talk about the second.

There is more than a little significance to Marx's observation that labor has become a commodity in our time and that, as a consequence, we are all somehow engaged in the selling of ourselves. It is not clear that Marx had a genuinely better scheme to advance. In what can only be called a Utopian fashion, he talks quite readily about a time when ordinary commercial relationships between us will no longer exist. "From each according to his ability, to each according to his need" would seem to characterize an ideal fraternal community or a family. Or heaven. Benjamin A. Rogge, a colleague of mine rather well known for his libertarian views, used to say with a smile that his family at dinner was the best example of socialism, adding, "He who brings in the most money does not necessarily take the largest pork chop." He thought it was the only situation in which the socialist ideal could be found.

It is probably time that we all come to recognize that there is no simple correlation between the wealth of some and the poverty of others. One cannot simply assert that some are poor because others are rich. Rockefeller used to say that his fortune distributed throughout the United States would make everybody a dime richer. There are societies in which everybody would have to be considered poor. Recent writings of Michael Novak and others have pointed to our kind of free enterprise society as that in which personal freedom and the greatest number of opportunities are available. Yet we must all be concerned about chronic unemployment and lack of education among many. Probably we do not need a new economic order. As Novak argues, the free market economy serves the overall community well. But it is hard to believe that we do not need new ways of behaving—such as would begin to transform the existing order.

"Profession" is a word which has come to signify virtually any person's life work. In the Middle Ages, however, there were essentially three professions: priesthood, law, and medicine; and the medieval understanding of "profession" is most compatible with the *Rule's* understanding of service. Professionals acquire an obligation, along with their skill, to use well the ability that is vital to the lives of others. Like most early thinkers, St. Benedict believed that one could determine a fair price for one's products. Present-day business people would not have approved of his well-meaning dictum that goods produced in the monastery should be sold at a little less than the going price. But how could one calculate the value of a service whose value is quite literally vital? As an example, how could I determine the value of the services of the one surgeon who can deal with my particular condition? There is an interesting moral force to the term "priceless" as used in regard to such a situation. The ideal was that the professional serves those who need him or her and is, in return, afforded a living. The living was to "keep them," as the old Presbyterian service of the calling of ministers used to say, "free from worldly care."

This notion was credible so long as most professionals were clerics, and it has survived for the longest time with respect to the Catholic priesthood. In terms of the loss of a moral ideal, it is regrettable that most Protestant ministers have for some time been salaried rather than afforded a living.

The almost universal availability of insurance has tended to mask the problem: when services are vital, what of the poor? An alternative form of the question might be: when the services are vital, who, needing them, will not become poor? We have become accustomed to thinking that we pay doctors, lawyers, (and ministers) for their services. Their own professional codes of conduct, however, still clearly indicate that their services should be afforded free to individuals who are incapable of paying for them. The *pro bono publico* work of the lawyer reflects this ideal. Public opinion polls suggest that many of us consider this an ideal more honored in the breach than in the observance. But we should be no harder on lawyers than on other professionals or on ourselves. How might we apply the service principle to the diverse employments in the world? To our own work?

"Vocation" is another term that has been used to characterize a person's lifework. It, too, has undergone considerable change as we have moved into the modern world. As early as Luther's time the word—it means "calling"—was used principally to refer to people in religious life: mostly monks and nuns. His transformation of the use of the term to the widest applications has always been deeply meaningful to me. Luther proposed that every person's work be considered a proper vocation. "Why," Martin Luther said, "a man could cobble shoes to the greater glory of God." The great scholar of the Church's social teaching, Ernst Troeltsch, suggested that because of this notion, which other reformers shared with Luther, the Reformation was "the clericization of the laity." Luther held that Christians should be Christ to one another.

In the orphanage in which he grew up, my father was taught the craft of a shoemaker and earned his living at it for most of his life. Simple Christian that he was, my father took immense care over his work: he took pride in it to the extent that he, indeed, wanted people to take him to be, in St. Paul's phrase, "A workman needing not to be ashamed." When customers came into his shop, my father showed them the shoes he had fixed, hoping for, indeed expecting, their approval. He worked in such a fashion that, knowing him to be a Christian, they would not think a Christian to be a poor workman. Without knowing about Luther, my father exemplified Luther's understanding of Christian vocation: "Cobbling shoes to the greater glory of God."

For those of us not in monastic life, the meaning of service in our time must lie somewhere between the professional's understanding of work and the craftsman's ideal of being a "workman needing not to be ashamed." Of course, we all assume that we must work to earn a living. And it is unrealistic to think that we could completely re-order our society so that we should not be "employed" and "employing." But we might achieve a community in which our work is understood as service offered the community, not simply as a way of earning a wage or salary. The monastery demonstrates the degree to which it is a real possibility.

If we commonly accepted the ideal of Christian service offered through ordinary work, there would be room for serious talk about the stewardship of what we derive from employment.

# XI

## RELIGION

### Reading from the *Rule:* chapter 62

Let them prefer nothing whatever to Christ, and may he bring us all together to everlasting life (*RB* 72:11–12).

With all of the recent talk of television evangelists, religion has tended to have something of a bad name among the media. The Tower of Babel would have interested them, as it represents religion as a human enterprise. When people are religious for the sake of manipulating God or the gods, they are superstitious; when they are engaged in religion for other purposes, they are often idolaters worshiping a nation, a class, a social dogma. We tend to overlook how much the Scriptures bring judgment upon false religion, on idolatry in particular. Thus it is only natural that St. Benedict would condemn gyrovagues and sarabaites. Their religion is idolatrous. In our own time, ''gyrovague'' would describe the individuals who drift from one religious cult to another, perhaps those who drift from one Christian denomination or parish to another.

Since St. Benedict speaks of false and unworthy religion at the opening of the *Rule,* it may appear surprising that there is little about formal observances of religion in the *Rule of St. Benedict.* If this is puzzling, it may be important to see what it is that we ourselves describe by the word.

We think of monks and nuns as "religious" and thus it may seem that the entirety of their lives must be, by definition, religious. This would seem to be in contrast to the lives of most of us, for we spend so much of our time in activities that apparently have little to do with religion, little connection with what we do when we go to church. They seem to be such contrasting activities that we think of "religion" as something different from what we think of as "life." The difference within our own lives is great; the difference between our lives and the lives of the "religious" is even greater.

Whatever differences exist, they are not defined by the presence or absence of religion. Because our activities are mostly in homes and workplaces, the time we spend in church seems to define for us the essence of religion as worship done in special places. We recognize that "being Christian" signifies that we try to live our lives in appropriate ways, but we incline to the view that "religion" is something different from "being religious." We even hear people saying things like, "Well, of course I am a Christian, but I'm not a very religious person." It is not entirely clear what people mean when they say things like this. At the very least, the words draw a distinction between everyday life and religious worship. This is, in fact, inappropriate and does not make sense in terms of the concerns of St. Benedict.

The community of which St. Benedict writes is in principle a lay phenomenon. We have become so accustomed to descriptions of monastic communities as being largely made up of priests or nuns that it comes as something of a surprise to discover that St. Benedict does not speak as if he is himself a priest. He is not a priest, and he makes it entirely clear that he does not regard the priestly office as a defining characteristic of membership in the community. The references to admitting priests as members of the monastery leave no doubt that he thinks they will tend to stir up the community with questions over precedence. And, in a day when formal education for the priesthood was not in existence, St. Benedict speaks almost offhandedly of a priest being ordained should one be needed.

Contemporary Benedictinism is reasserting this position: in principle the monastic community is made up of laypersons. Once monsticism had become established in the West, it would have been assumed that any intelligent young man entering the monastery—perhaps anyone not coming from the peasant class—would be a candidate in due time for ordination. Indeed, for many years, "choir monk" and "ordained monk" seemed equivalent terms. Today in many communities, both ordained and unordained monks are addressed as "brother," perhaps with the exception of the abbot's being called "father." All of this emphasizes the lay ideal of St. Benedict.

The Rule of the Master, which we have mentioned a number of times as the document which lies behind the *Rule of St. Benedict*, even suggests that the Eucharist was not celebrated within the monastery—as if the Master's monks may have gone elsewhere to receive the sacrament, perhaps to the village church. The Master also refers to the abbot distributing "blessed bread" in the monastery, although he is not a priest.

St. Benedict does not go into any greater detail about any of this, but he implies that the abbot is not ordained. There is no clear reference in the *Rule* to the time or manner of celebrating Eucharist, although the receiving of Holy Communion is mentioned in *RB* 63.4. But St. Benedict's mention of the Eucharist implies something of what we have been calling the "religious" nature of the monastic life.

Of peculiar significance in all this is the possibility of having a life so completely devoted to the work of God that "religion" as we ordinarily think of it hardly needs to be mentioned. For centuries we have witnessed the misunderstanding of "religion"—as if it were a department of life alongside one's work and other activities. To some degree it may be that the rise of monasticism led to this misunderstanding. Monastics seemed so religious to the layperson—even to the extent that their life was called "religion" or "religious life"—that the layperson's life could only be thought of as something else. In the same way, we have also come to distinguish the religious aspects of our lives from the secular.

Our religious rituals are for the great interim between the resurrection and ascension of our Lord and the final conclusion of creation in the new heaven and the new earth. Our Lord himself says during the Last Supper that he will not again partake of earthly food until he partakes of it anew with the Father.

We need, perhaps, to recall that in the heavenly city of John's Revelation there is no temple. Why would it be needed? Similarly, when the whole of life is devoted to God, it is not necessary to have a separate compartment that is for the worship of God. The monastics' time in the abbey church is not specially religious because they are in the place of community prayer and celebration. Their study and their work are no less acts of worship for being done in cells or fields or workshops.

And we can immediately see that the same orientation is possible in our secular lives. Our work, our family relationships, all that we are can be so dedicated to God that there is no compartmentalization of religion. When we gather to worship, we gather to acknowledge that the entirety of life is the form of our devotion, that it can be this and should be this.

A consequence of this attitude should be a better understanding of the nature of ministry in the Church. The ordained ministry of the Church would no longer be regarded as having the sole responsibility for exemplifying religion. We are all called to be dedicated to God in every aspect of our lives.

We have suggested two things: that religion is not a department of life alongside life's other activities and that ministry is not the preserve of only some of us. It is the call of all of us.

We do not have to be silly in the conclusions we draw from this. There are, of course, sacramental functions in the life of the Church, and it is appropriate that there be persons specially trained and authorized to carry out these functions. Even the radical Protestants, who at the time of the Reformation were most opposed to the Catholic understanding of the sacraments, tended to think it appropriate that the function of the Church in worship should be the special concern of properly trained individuals. But much in the way that Luther wanted to say that all Christians have vocations, we might say that we are all called to Christian ministry, although we are not all called to the same ministry.

In the small village in which we lived during the Second World War (having been bombed out of our London home), there was a strange man whose special job it was to pump the organ in the parish church. Although this would not seem to be a particularly difficult job, it was very hard work, and everyone could immediately hear when it was not being done well. Reg did his job well and took it very seriously. As the time for a service approached, he could be seen walking down the village high street, usually carrying a piece of organ music under his arm. An acquaintance of mine once called out to him, "Hello, Reg! On your way to play your concerto on the bellows, eh?" I don't recall how Reg responded. But I have often thought about him since. He had a vocation that few of us wanted and likely few of us could discharge well. His was a significant form of Christian ministry, clearly related to worship in God's house. Is mine any less a vocation, any less a form of Christian ministry?

In fact, all the things that are done by Christian people are forms of Christian ministry. We are fairly prompt to think that being a good surgeon might be a form of ministry, perhaps teaching. But think about Reg and his colleagues in life. That, too, is ministry, as is my washing of the dishes.

We are, as St. Benedict reminds us, preparing for a life when we shall all dwell in the presence of God. And life then will clearly be the worship of God. And we have anticipated what that New Age must be by seeing its foreshadowing in the life of St. Benedict's community.

# XII

## THE END AS BEGINNING

### Reading from the *Rule:* chapters 1, 73

Are you hastening toward your heavenly home? Then with Christ's help, keep this little rule that we have written for beginners. After that, you can set out for the loftier summits of the teaching and virtues we mentioned above, and under God's protection you will reach them. Amen (*RB* 73:8–9).

The short chapter ending *The Rule of St. Benedict* is entitled "This Rule Only a Beginning of Perfection." Many have felt that this chapter suggests an attitude on the part of St. Benedict critical of the cenobitic life. It is, for them, as if—after setting out a rule for life in the monastery—St. Benedict indicates that there is something better. Was it the life of the hermit? With due respect to many distinguished thinkers, such a view does not seem to square with his praise of the cenobite in the opening pages of the *Rule*. It does not seem to me necessary to find a contradiction between what St. Benedict writes here and what precedes it.

For many who read it for the first time, the *Rule of St. Benedict* suggests standards that are altogether too demanding. Perhaps the only way in which one might hope to meet its implied demands *is* by entering a community in which there would be a constant reminder of the practice of humility and so on. Yet we have found that the *Rule's* demands are frequently constructed in recognition of human fallibility and human needs. This in turn has led to thoughts about the ways in which St. Benedict's recommendations could apply to the lives of persons living in the ordinary circles of human society, with all of the ways in which they intersect. Monks and nuns today are more likely to vote in elections than the average person on the outside, and perhaps there are, as a consequence, some who see conflicts between living a cloistered life and voicing concern about the issues that confront all citizens of a democratic society. So too, there are, for us, the intersections of the lives of spouses and children, of our lives as supervisors and supervised, of the many societies and clubs in which people concerned for their society will participate.

Acknowledging these complexities, we have given thought to the ways in which reading St. Benedict leads to consideration of the kinds of practical actions and aspirations that might significantly affect our lives.

Given the multiple claims which we experience in life, we have realized that it would be well for us to sort out which influences affect us through a kind of duress and which are genuine authorities. For example, we rarely find that we have quite sufficient funds in any week or year to do all of the things which we should like to accomplish. Our felt need to improve our financial situation is the most pressing need which many of us experience, even as we recognize that there are poorer people for whom that pressure must be almost unbelievably greater. Yet we discover that we are able to distinguish between the great pressures which we feel and the claims which are genuine—authoritative—demands placed upon us.

There is the person who has been elected or appointed to some civic body and who could gain ready popularity by espousing some cause but who recognizes that truth or honor or some other high value requires a different course of action. As John Bunyan's *Pilgrim's Progress* reminds us, once we have started upon the road to popularity, it is increasingly difficult to turn aside from it, whereas the person who started off to make decisions by a higher standard becomes stronger in doing the right.

We are prone to suggest that we live in a society in which all persons are free to do whatever is legally right for them; yet we recognize that such a society is on a dangerous and slippery slope unless some are moved by a legitimate claim upon them which they acknowledge and are willing to honor. As Alan Donagan points out in his book strikingly called *The Theory of Morality*, a society entirely made up of people willing to be no more than moral would be singularly unlovely. A genuine community requires people to be more than merely moral, merely law abiding. Generosity is one characteristic that he mentions.

It is obvious that infanticide and enthanasia are but a short step from widespread abortion. The one must be resisted or none can. But a pluralist society will not make such resistance particularly enjoyable: pluralism is power devoid of authority.

So it is significant that St. Benedict calls us to think about the nature of authority in our lives, and, while not being cloistered persons, we resolve to live to honor the authority that stems from God.

Thinking of the tools of society and the consequences of humility in human relationships, we are bound to use the tests implied by the *Rule* to judge the relationships we have with other human beings, both those within our immediate family and the people with whom we are daily in contact in our work and in our society.

We cannot fail to notice that the nature of interpersonal relationships that stem from the *Rule* tends to run counter to those that are recommended to individuals anxious for success in their work or their society. To be sure, there is much talk about nurturing behavior, but it becomes quite clear to us that many who profess to be our friends are basically desiring of our votes. The person coming from an Old World culture cannot fail to be impressed by the ready tendency we have in America to address quite casual acquaintances by their first names. I was struck, when visiting my sister in England some years ago, to note that she continued to address her neighbor by her married name—after twenty years of living next door. Surely we should be naive to think that every person who calls us by our first name is in a transformed relationship with us. The law school that recently boasted that its faculty and students addressed one another by their first names failed to comment on the fact that students are still dependent upon the judgment of the faculty whose first names they are encouraged to pronounce.

St. Benedict's teaching concerning humility has persuaded us that what is needed is transformed relationships, a matter profoundly more difficult to achieve than the cosmetic of seeming friendliness.

From St. Benedict we have learned that genuine concern will require that relationships transcend pleasantries and techniques, and we find ourselves resolving to live together in a more profoundly human fashion than newspaper columnists can afford to recommend.

When, after many years of living in the city, my wife and I finally moved to the small town where we now live, we slept rather poorly for the first couple of nights. We concluded that it was because the nights in Crawfordsville are quiet by contrast with what had become familiar to us in Chicago. "That strange noise you hear is quiet." In so many ways the *Rule* calls upon us to set aside all of the stimulation which, in our contemporary world, is often viewed as the only means by which a person can avoid total boredom. What is to be said about a situation in which people wishing to be, as they tend to say, "on good terms with their bodies" and thus committed to exercising each day, do so not listening to birds and other natural sounds, but listening rather to some kind of music on their headsets?

Many of the great spiritual teachers of the Church have verified that we begin to make progress toward God as we learn to accept ourselves as we are. St. Benedict has caused us to reflect upon the fact that as the psalms call us to come to terms with ourselves as creatures before God, so prayer and silence teach us to avoid the kinds of stimulation that are themselves an avoidance of genuine personhood.

Giving even the slightest attention to St. Benedict calls us to reflect upon our situation in life: our relative well being as compared with so many of our contemporaries in this world and the capacity we have to contribute to the needy among whom we live. With even the slightest encouragement from the *Rule*, we have started to think of what it was that we could actually share from the goods we have, what we might actually contribute of our services to people who could benefit from them. One of the most incredible organizations I have ever seen is the Christian Nursing Service, which was started in Crawfordsville by a group of retired nurses who had taken upon themselves a concern for needy people, particularly needy infants. Not depending in any way on government financing, it was a rediscovery of Christian charity, which many of us could only desire to emulate. From a modest beginning, it has grown into a number of other services, most recently a hospice.

As we have thought about these matters, we have begun to think that we might attempt to follow aspects of the monastic life as they could be expressed in our lives in the world. Doubtless we have recognized that this would take quite a bit of determination and still be fairly difficult to accomplish. But we discover that, as we come to the end of this examination of the *Rule's* relevance to our lives, we can still only be at the beginning.

What set me thinking about the *Rule* and visiting monasteries was the consequences of my having said to a monk some years ago that I thought I was beginning to understand what led people to undertake such a form of life. He suggested that I really had a great deal yet to learn. After the passage of these years, I realize how true his statement was. Thirty years later, there is still a great deal to learn.

Yet we are constantly tempted to think that we are truly "in the Way," as early Christians used to say. And we are constantly discovering that one of the most difficult things to avoid in the Christian life is this notion that we are really quite accomplished and experienced Christians. It is our foolish but utterly human tendency to strive to be humble and then find that we have a sneaking regard for the fact that we are getting better at being humble. It is quite difficult—isn't it?—to work out the reverse logic involved. If we were becoming *more* humble, we should be thinking that we are less humble than we ought to be. And wouldn't that realization then be a source of some satisfaction for us?

In the *Screwtape Letters*, Lewis has Screwtape (a kind of district sales manager among devils) writing to Wormwood (who is new on the job) to say that he needs to get the Christian assigned to him to begin to take pride in the fact that he is getting more humble. Our problem! Screwtape acknowledges ruefully, however, that occasionally the Christian will recognize the absurdity of the situation and laugh over the idea of being proud of being humble. And when that happens, Screwtape notes, Wormwood has lost control of the situation and has to start all over again.

That we tend to take ourselves too seriously is the reason why the end is ever only a beginning where the school of Christ is concerned. In fact, this life of the Christian is truly like that of the student, and we are truly as St. Benedict said—in school. Like students, the early part of our life is very much taken up with concern about "how we are doing." It is difficult for students, when first they learn about the existence of grading, not to be concerned about getting good grades. But as we mature as students, we come to be wrapped up with the subject itself, so that the business of grades is rarely considered. So long as it is a matter of grades, we are not very far advanced.

The experienced monks whom I have referred to in this

book strike me as students who have gotten beyond a concern for grades and have discovered that the real reason for being in school is that the subject matter is itself of all-absorbing significance. To ask them how they are doing with respect to humility would seem a little like asking Vladimir Horowitz how his scales are coming along.

At first, we turn to religion for peace of mind or for a variety of other reasons. At last, we realize that the only reason for following the Christian life is that it leads to God. Perhaps it is something of a play on words, yet it is accurate to say that understanding God as the end of our life as Christians is the beginning of our maturity as Christians. And to recognize that we are on this path is to know that God's grace so far exceeds our capacity to comprehend it that we are ever only at the beginning of the path.

As we say to ourselves that we should like to be making just a little progress, the pride in humility business starts all over again. But any progress we make along this path is finally not our own doing at all but is the work of the grace of God in our lives coming to be manifest to us (see *RB* 4.42).

In fact, we have not the slightest idea of how far we have progressed on this our path to God, nor of how long we have to pursue it. "Our times are in his hands." The important matter is that we are pursuing our chief end, which is, as the *Shorter Catechism of the Westminster Confession* puts it, "to glorify God and enjoy him forever." If we are glorifying God, it seems quite foolish to wonder if we are doing it well or if we are getting any better at it. We shall ever only be God's creatures reflecting God's glory, so it is foolish to think that we shall want to give ourselves credit at any point.

Even so, God knows what foolish creatures we are and wills to humor us. Thus the wise master, St. Benedict, ends his *Rule* with a little chiding—reminding us that we are slothful, unobservant, and negligent (and we must readily acknowledge that we are)—but offers kind words of comfort in conclusion:

> Are you hastening to your heavenly home? Then with Christ's help, keep this little rule that we have written for beginners. After that, you can set out for the loftier summits of the teaching and virtues we mentioned above, and under God's protection you will reach them. Amen (*RB* 73.8-9).

It is with such a promise in mind that we pilgrims are marching toward the heavenly city in company with St. Benedict and his sons and daughters of all the centuries.

# BIBLIOGRAPHY

The following are some relatively non-technical books that are either recently published or are classics readily available from a library.

Boulding, Maria, ed. *A Touch of God*. Still River, Mass.: St. Bede's Publications, 1983 (reprint of SPCK edition, 1982).

Butler, Cuthbert. *Benedictine Monachism*. Cambridge: Speculum Historale, 1961 (reprint of Longman's edition of 1924).

de Vogue, Adalbert. *The Rule of Saint Benedict*. Kalamazoo: Cistercian Publications, 1983.

de Waal, Esther. *Seeking God: The Way of St. Benedict*. Collegeville: The Liturgical Press, 1984.

Griffiths, Bede. *The Golden String*. Garden City, N.Y.: Doubleday, 1964.

Knowles, David. *Christian Monasticism*. New York: McGraw-Hill, 1969 (reprinted 1977).

Leclercq, Jean. *The Love of Learning and the Desire for God*. New York: New American Library, 1962.

*Monastic Studies*, "On Benedictine Monasticism," Mount Savior, N.Y.: Mount Savior Monastery, 1975.

Zarnecki, George. *The Monastic Achievement*. New York: McGraw-Hill, 1972.

The following books, additional to those mentioned above, are mentioned in the text:

*The Letters of Abelard and Heloise*. New York: Penguin Books, 1974.

Alan Bloom. *The Closing of the American Mind*. New York: Simon & Schuster, 1987.

Alan Donagan. *The Theory of Morality.* Chicago: University of Chicago Press, 1977.

Fyodor Dostoyevsky. *The Brothers Karamazov.*

C.S. Lewis. *Reflections on the Psalms.* New York: Harcourt Brace Jovanovich, 1958.

_____. *The Screwtape Letters.* New York: Macmillan, 1962.

Alasdair MacIntyre. *After Virtue.* Notre Dame: University of Notre Dame Press, 1984.

George Orwell. *The Road to Wigan Pier.*

Ernst Troeltsch. *The Social Teachings of the Christian Churches.* London: George Allen and Unwin, 1931.